Twayne's English Authors Series

EDITOR OF THIS VOLUME

Arthur F. Kinney

University of Massachusetts, Amherst

Barnabe Googe

TEAS 306

Coat of arms from Googe's translation of *The Popish Kingdome, or Reigne of Antichrist*, by Thomas Naogeorgus (1570). (*Reproduced by permission of* The Huntington Library, *San Marino, California*)

BARNABE GOOGE

By William E. Sheidley

University of Connecticut

TWAYNE PUBLISHERS
A DIVISION OF G. K. HALL & CO., BOSTON

Published in 1981 by Twayne Publishers,
A Division of G. K. Hall & Co.
All Rights Reserved

Printed on permanent/durable acid-free paper and bound
in the United States of America

First Printing

Library of Congress Cataloging in Publication Data

Sheidley, William E
Barnabe Googe.

(Twayne's English authors series ; TEAS 306)
Bibliography: p. 144
Includes index.
1.   Googe, Barnabe, 1540–1594—Criticism and
interpretation.
PR2279.G4Z88   1981   821'.3   80-28043
ISBN 0-8057-6798-3

In Memoriam
B.E.S. & E.W.W.

Contents

Editor's Note

Barnabe Googe has long been known as the author of some important early eclogues and lyrics that are essential to our understanding of the growth of English poetry during the Renaissance. In the first book-length study of Googe's work, William E. Sheidley demonstrates the variety of Googe's achievement by stressing his work as a translator as well as a poet and arguing that, along with George Gascoigne, his is a central and important voice of the mid-sixteenth century. Googe emerges here as occupying a vital station between the early Tudor poetry under Henry VIII and the flowering of the great poets under Elizabeth I.

—Arthur F. Kinney

About the Author

William E. Sheidley is Associate Professor of English at the University of Connecticut, where he has taught since 1966. He received his Ph.D. from Stanford University in 1968. From 1973 through 1978 he was Co-Editor of the scholarly annual *Children's Literature*. His published writings include essays on English Renaissance poetry in *Journal of English and Germanic Philology, Concerning Poetry, Studies in English Literature, Modern Philology, Studies in Philology,* and *Modern Language Quarterly.*

Preface

Obscured from the view of subsequent generations by the towering achievements of their immediate successors, English writers of the 1560s and 1570s have received mostly cursory study and desultory appreciation. When the early Elizabethans are noticed at all, it is usually by relation to some development that culminates outside their era: they introduce Senecan tragedy, bridge the gap between Surrey and Sidney, regularize English prosody, or begin the translation movement that matures in the later work of North and Chapman. Barnabe Googe is no exception. Known to some for his eclogues because they precede *The Shepheardes Calender*, to others for his lyrics because they fit a theory of the evolution of styles, and to still others for his translations because they help scholars read Spenser and Shakespeare, Googe is familiar to practically none as a characteristic and leading literary man of his own epoch.

In fact, he not only produced a group of translated and original works that embodies the essential literary culture of his generation; he also developed a distinctive literary personality which, while rooted in that culture, transcends it. The purpose of this study is to define Googe's identity as a writer by surveying all his various works in their own context and to assess his contribution at large. Although the chapters that follow make no claim to advance him to major stature, they do express the conviction that a clear and complete view of his canon reveals Googe to be, apart from Gascoigne, the most interesting and significant of the early Elizabethan poets.

After tracing the vicissitudes of Googe's reputation through four centuries, Chapter 1 offers a short account of his life and career and a few words on one of the main barriers to appreciation of his work, the peculiar modes of prosody and style fashionable in his time. Chapter 2 studies *The Zodiake of Life*, which Googe translated from the Renaissance Latin of Palingenius, explaining why Googe and his contemporaries regarded such a work as his masterpiece. Chapters 3 and 4 explore the works of Googe most highly regarded today, his short poems, as well as his eclogues, his dream vision, and his long moral poem. Here the goal is to establish their relation to Googe's own literary problems and projects—that is, to place them in their time—before attempting to determine to what extent they live beyond it. The account of "The Ship of Safegarde" marks the first time this interesting work has been fully discussed in print. Chapter 5 concludes the study, as Googe ended his career, with a miscellany of translations. Although his fame is diminished by the degree to which the value awarded translation has decreased, Googe's choice of works to "english" and his mode of translating them express his poetic intentions and the taste of his times just as well as would an equivalent shelf of original works.

Such insight into Googe and his writings as this study attains depends largely on the contribution of previous scholars and critics, and I have tried to acknowledge my indebtedness in the notes and in the text. On one work in particular I have relied at every turn, the unpublished 1954 Harvard dissertation by Brooke Peirce, "Barnabe Googe: Poet and Translator." Professor Peirce has generously given me permission to use his study, which contains the only modern biography of Googe and a thorough description of his works.

I have received liberal support for this project from the University of Connecticut Research Foundation and have relied on the indispensable assistance of the staff of the University of Connecticut Library, as well, on occasion, as that of the Huntington Library, the Houghton Library, and the library of the Hispanic Society of America.

The index was prepared by Kathleen McCormick.

Section II of Chapter 4 is adapted from my article, "A Timely Anachronism: Tradition and Theme in Barnabe Googe's 'Cupido Conquered,'" in *Studies in Philology*, Volume 69, No. 2, © 1972 The University of North Carolina Press.

Nancy M. Fairbanks, Judith M. Kennedy, and Brooke Peirce have painstakingly criticized the entire manuscript. They provided various other kinds of help and encouragement as well, as did Raymond A. Anselment, Sylvia E. Bowman, Bennett A. Brockman, Joseph Cary, A. Harris Fairbanks, Lee A. Jacobus, Karen K. Jambeck, Thomas J. Jambeck, Arthur F. Kinney, Lawrence V. Ryan, Robert M. Schuler, and especially my wife, Harlow W. Sheidley. For the completion of this book and for whatever merits it may possess, these and other colleagues, teachers, and friends are largely responsible; its shortcomings, of course, arise from my own.

WILLIAM E. SHEIDLEY

University of Connecticut
Storrs, Connecticut

Chronology

1540   Barnabe Googe born, eldest son of Robert Goche of Lincoln-shire and Margaret Mantell of Kent. Margaret dies soon after his birth. Googe is to spend at least part of his childhood at the home of his maternal grandmother, Lady Hales, in Kent.

1552   Robert Goche marries the daughter of a London goldsmith and acquires lands and offices in Lincolnshire.

1555   Googe matriculates pensioner, Christ's College, Cambridge.

1557   Upon the death of his father, Googe becomes an unsold ward of the court.

1558   Googe begins translating *The Zodiake of Life*, by Palingenius, but leaves off in despair of success.

1559   Now residing at Staple Inn in London, Googe resumes work on the *Zodiake*.

1560   Googe first appears in print with a prefatory poem in an anti-Papist volume. Shortly thereafter, his translation of the first three books of the *Zodiake* is published.

1561   Still residing at Staple Inn, Googe publishes the first six books of the *Zodiake*, dedicated to Sir William Cecil, Master of Wards. Googe is allowed to purchase his own wardship. He travels to France and Spain with the embassade of Sir Thomas Challoner, returning home in 1562.

1563   *Eglogs, Epytaphes, and Sonettes* is published. Googe becomes embroiled in a controversy over his engagement to Mary Darrell of Kent that Archbishop Parker resolves in his favor, at Cecil's behest. Although he is given license to enter upon his lands, most of Googe's revenue remains under the control of his stepmother.

1564   Googe marries Mary Darrell February 5, and, apparently settling in Kent, begins rearing a family that will eventually include eight children.

1565   The complete translation of the *Zodiake* is published.

1569   *The Shippe of Safegarde* is published, dedicated from London to Googe's wife's younger sisters on February 14.

1570   Googe's translation of *The Popish Kingdome* by Thomas Naogeorgus is published.

1571   Googe's patron and kinsman Cecil is created the first Baron Burghley.

1572   Googe attends at Queen Elizabeth's visit to Burghley's manor Theobalds. Googe's grandmother and benefactor, Lady Hales, dies.

1574   Burghley sends Googe to Ireland to report on Essex's expedition against Ulster. He stays six months, returning with commendation from Essex in July.

1576   Residing in Kingston-upon-Hull in Kent, Googe revises the *Zodiake* for a new edition, dedicated to Burghley.

1577   Googe's translations of *The Overthrow of the Gout* by Christopher Balista and *Fovre Bookes of Husbandry* by Conrad Heresbach are published. Googe is evidently engaged in farming and raising medicinal herbs.

1578   Googe supports the idea of a standing army in a prose preface to the *Allarme to England* by Barnabe Riche, whom he knew in Ireland.

1579   Googe's translation of *The Prouerbes* from the Spanish of the Marqués of Santillana is published.

1581   Googe serves at the court banquet in honor of French emissaries. At this period he waits daily on Burghley.

1582   Googe, in financial distress, returns to Ireland to become Provost Marshal of the Presidency Court of Connaught.

1583   In September, Googe returns to England temporarily.

1584   Googe's stepmother dies, releasing his patrimony of lands in Lincolnshire. Legal delays make it necessary for him to resort to Ireland in September.

1585   Googe sells his Irish office and retires to England in April.

1587   Googe is at court in June and at home in Alvingham, Lincolnshire, in August. His translation of a pamphlet on a drug, "Terra Sigillata," is published.

1594   Googe dies at Alvingham in February.

CHAPTER 1

Barnabe Googe in His Time— and Afterwards

O N an early winter evening, a young scholar sits among his books, huddling against the cold. To his astonishment, suddenly the Nine Muses sweep into view, "with stately steps/ . . . In Mantels grate of comely grace." He falls to the floor before them but is unceremoniously commanded to stand up and get to work. After Melpomene orders him to translate Lucan and Urania requests him to undertake Aratus, Calliope begs that she may instead employ him to make Palingenius, who "did trede the crabbed wayes, / Of vertuous lyfe," accessible to "the meane and ruder sorte." The proposition is readily approved by all save the scholar, who pleads incapacity and asks to be excused for fear of incurring "immortall shame." But the Muse is a hard mistress, and with her sisters she frowns severely on any hesitation by her servant:

> Take thou this same in hande thei crie
>   thou hast none other choyse.
> And fast a way from me thei flyng,
>   as halfe in angrye moode.[1]

So Barnabe Googe, age nineteen, portrays himself at the inauguration of his literary career: "as vnto learnyng thrall" (sig. °6v), aware of the laughable presumption inherent in pairing himself with the Muses' darlings by translating their works, nervous about the critical reception that might await his efforts, but convinced of the moral utility and importance of the job. As it happened, his translation of Marcellus Palingenius's *Zodiake of Life* won Googe substantial praise from his contemporaries, and his claim to inspiration for an assemblage of commonplace moral philosophy from the Muse of epic poetry—the highest form—reflects the taste of his generation. But posterity has more uniformly borne out Googe's fear that "In England here a hundred

15

headdes / more able now therebe" for writing poetry worthy of lasting fame.

A few years later Googe reported another discussion of his literary career with a supernatural visitor, this time Mercury, who guides him through his dream vision in "Cupido Conquered." As before, Googe acknowledges the incongruity of his trafficking with the famous figures of classical literature by making himself the butt of humor. Speechless at first, he finally stammers out:

> Thou Goddesse Son, why standste y^u there
>   what busines now w^t thee,
> What meanest y^u in thy flying weed,
>   For to appeare to me. . . .

Mercury replies that the Muses, grateful for his previous labors, have sent him to help and encourage the poet, who has been stung by "*Momus* ill report."[2] Even the greatest English writers of the day— Norton, Phaer, Baldwin, Neville—have been criticized. As for Googe, "The day shall come," Mercury assures him, "when thankfull men, / shall well accept thy Paine" (p. 147). That day has been slow to dawn. Googe was judiciously respected in his own time, but before he died in 1594 the age had long since passed when the names listed above marked the highest standard of attainment in English letters.

I   *Googe's Literary Reputation*

Almost entirely forgotten for over a hundred years, Googe and his works were exhumed by eighteenth- and nineteenth-century antiquarians and bibliophiles.[3] Thomas Warton's matter-of-fact account set the tone for subsequent literary historians, whose distaste for Googe's writings is imperfectly hidden by scattered bits of grudging praise.[4] For some, Googe presented an opportunity to vent scholarly impatience or critical scorn. A speaker in Collier's *Poetical Decameron* remarks that Googe, "though a voluminous writer, and especially translator, has produced nothing original that I have ever seen worth preserving."[5] Rollins and Baker, although they give him generous space in their anthology, cannot refrain from observing that "Googe's first impulse to let his juvenilia lie in darkness was probably sound."[6] Perhaps Googe's reputation hits rock-bottom in Don Cameron Allen's devastating epithet, "subpoet."[7]

But however repellent to refined sensibilities, Googe's works have had an undeniable value to historical scholarship. Long before Rollins and Baker recognized in the collection of short poems "a grim little testimonial to the continuing influence of Tottel's *Miscellany*,"[8] the diligent Edward Arber in 1871 had reprinted it with introduction and notes as an important link in the chain of English poetry, calling Googe one of "the heralds, the forerunners, the teachers of Spenser, Shakespeare, and Johnson [*sic*]."[9] Shortly thereafter, an elegant facsimile of one translation appeared,[10] and Googe, thus accessible, began to attract the attention of specialists. To the student of Spanish influence on English literature, for example, he was important as the first Elizabethan to reflect it; for the historian of the pastoral, he offered the only clear anticipation of *The Shepheardes Calender* in English; for the scholar in quest of sources for ideas and images in Shakespeare and Spenser, the *Zodiake* provided a major repository; and for the writer interested in the influence of works Googe translated, he served as a crucial conduit.

It is mostly to critics interested specifically in the history of the short poem, however, that Googe owes his partial rehabilitation during the present century. As early as 1905, John Erskine saw in many of Googe's poems what he held indispensable to the successful lyric, an honest expression of personal feeling.[11] To Yvor Winters, whose essay on the Renaissance lyric has commanded attention for over forty years, Googe formed an important stage in the native tradition of the plain style.[12] Writers following Winters's suggestions have analyzed Googe's lyrics and their historical context with a care befitting works of stature, and the poems have been edited and anthologized, so that today they surely reach a wider and more appreciative audience than when they were first published.[13]

Although occasionally his original works were acknowledged,[14] among his contemporaries Googe was mainly famous as a translator.[15] Translation was the distinctive literary activity of Googe's generation, which labored to fill the empty shelves of the English library by the readiest expedient and to mesh the vernacular culture of England with the neo-Latin culture of Renaissance Europe at large.[16] Most of the writers with whom Googe is associated were primarily translators, whether of Seneca's tragedies, Mantuan's eclogues, or Homer from the French. Many entered the service of the Protestant statesmen and clerics who had come to power with Elizabeth, just as Googe himself joined the household of his kinsman Sir William Cecil, later Lord Burghley.[17]

Their literary labors were designed to advance the general program of the new regime, which included purging the realm of vice, papistry, and dissension while educating the populace to the need for civil order, obedience, and a patriotism focused on the crown. In this context, "englishing" a foreign classic was a service to the nation—all the more so if it contained sound moral doctrine, Protestant polemic, or useful practical information. As for narrative poetry or the lyric, though it was well to demonstrate that English was as good a tongue for a sonnet[18] as Italian or French, one had carefully to avoid seeming to espouse idleness or vice.

Under the influence of the rhetorical education they received at the hands of an older generation of humanists, Googe and his fellows believed in the power of poetry to move the mind to virtue;[19] unlike the younger group of writers who supplanted them in the middle of their lives, however, their interest was always engaged more in the purpose being pursued than in the poetry itself. Their writings frequently have a rough-and-ready quality that makes them seem naive and rustic in comparison with the sophisticated craftsmanship of Sidney or Spenser. Caught thus between a paternal establishment whose projects and values served as their own and the advent of a brilliant new generation that would redefine English literary culture in less constrictive terms, most writers born in the 1530s and 1540s gave up original poetry quickly—if they ever tried it—and lapsed into virtual silence before 1580.[20]

Googe's career provides a definitive example of this pattern, and, thanks to autobiographical remarks in his prefaces and texts and to a number of letters and official records that have been preserved, it is possible to reconstruct it in some detail.[21] The picture that emerges offers insights into the interplay of ambition, learning, and personal awareness that generates literary art, and it provides a window on life at the fringes of power during the first half of Elizabeth's reign.

II A Brief Life of Googe

Barnabe Googe was born in 1540, perhaps on St. Barnabas' Day (June 11), either in Lincolnshire or in Kent.[22] His father, Robert Goche,[23] held official posts in the vicinity of Lincoln as early as 1547 and acquired land in Alvingham in 1552,[24] but it is not clear that he resided there when his son was born. On June 18, 1539, Robert had married Margaret Mantell in Beakesborne, Kent; she died almost immediately after Barnabe's birth a year later. The child evidently spent a good deal of his youth at Dungeon, the manor in Kent where his maternal grandmother resided with her third husband, Sir James Hales. Googe dedicated his first book to her, "not as a recompence for youre manyfolde benefite, but rather as a sygne of my vnfayned good will, and bounden duety" (*Zodiake*, 1560, sig. °3), and confesses himself urged to the work by a cluster of Kentish relatives and friends, including John Bale, then canon and prebendary of Canterbury Cathedral.[25] Years later he recalled her virtue, charity, and hospitality in a loving portrait of this "very *Phoenix* and *Parageon*" of gentlewomen that he interpolated along with other remarks on the people and places of Kent in his version of Conrad Heresbach's *Fovre Bookes of Husbandry*.[26]

In 1552 Googe's father married Ellen Gadbury, the daughter of a London goldsmith, and soon purchased estates in Lincolnshire. Upon his death in 1557, however, Googe, still a minor, became an unsold ward of the court, and even after he was allowed to purchase his own wardship in 1561 and given license to enter upon his lands in 1563, his patrimony remained mostly at the disposal of the woman he referred to as his "lewd mother-in-law" until her death in 1584.[27] If Thomas Wilson is to be believed, Googe had reason to be grateful even for so conditional a release from dependency. The rhetorician writes: "In lamenting the miserye of wardeshyppes, I might saie it is not for noughte so communely said: I wil handle you like a warde."[28] For his good fortune Googe could thank his "cousin" Cecil, newly appointed Master of Wards in 1561,[29] who had already helped his father and who readily welcomed his orphaned young kinsman into his circle of retainers.[30]

It was natural for Googe to attach himself to the leader of the Protestant faction surrounding Elizabeth. He was allied by family ties and other associations to many of the exiles of the 1550s and those who supported them,[31] and both his stepgrandfather Sir James Hales and the poet Nicholas Grimald whom he admired enough to eulogize were hounded into recantation.[32] To a young poet seeking a place under the new queen, the sufferings undergone by his elders would have constituted the single most important fact of life in the world. Googe attended Christ's College, Cambridge (matriculated as a pensioner, 1555),[33] a center of reform, during the height of the Marian persecutions. Many of the martyrs had studied, preached, or taught at Cambridge, and Googe himself might even have seen John Hullier perish

at the stake in Jesus Green in 1556.[34] Although Cambridge later
became a hotbed of anti-Anglican puritanism, the effect of Googe's
experiences there was simply to confirm him in the anti-Papist nation-
alism of his day. He had a chance to act on his convictions in the 1580s
when as a colonial official in Ireland he could confiscate the natives'
breviaries and "solemn servysses of our Lady,"[35] and he voiced his
attitude repeatedly in his writings, beginning with his first appearance
in print.

Indeed, his six poulter's distichs commending the translation of an
attack on the Pope by Nilus Cabasilas, a ninth-century Metropolitan of
Thessalonica, introduce themes that were to occupy him during his
whole career.[36] Googe's classical education had taught him to venerate
the works of the ancients; his political affiliations and family connections gave him reason to hate and fear the Roman church. What luck
to find one of those very ancients—or a fair approximation of one—
attacking the modern enemy! And how easy and natural to represent
the conflict in terms of the standard polarity between spirit and flesh,
virtue and worldly indulgence, that would ever serve as the moral
compass of Googe's poetic universe. It is a promising debut. Googe
weaves a border of repellent associations around the stock charge that
the Roman church has usurped secular power, centering it on the
emblem of "that hauty whoore" of Babylon, and then contravenes
Rome's claim to the authority of greater antiquity over the new
denominations by enlisting the ancient eastern prelate in the Protestant
cause. I quote it here in full because it has not elsewhere been
reprinted:

> Let rankour not you rule,
> O men of Romyshe secte:
> Expell the poyson frō your brests
> That dothe you thus infecte.
>   Let not that hauty whoore
> That boasts her selfe for god:
> That rules the realms of Cesars right
> With her vsurped rod:
> Let not this hag I say,
> Bewitche your earthly eyes:
> That here embraceth beastly ioye,
> And vertue dooth despyse.
>   Antiquitie she sayth,
> Gaue her this stately place:

Lo here Antiquitie you see
Dothe her and hers deface.
  Lo here dothe Nilus teache,
A man of ancient tyme
Howe muche she is to be abhorde,
Howe muche she swelles with crime.
  Leaue her therfore in tyme
Forsake her wicked wayes:
Let vs and you agree in one,
So God shall haue his prayse.

The book in which this poem appears was printed on March 16, 1560; its translator, Thomas Gressop, is identified as a "student in Oxforde." Googe himself was by then living in London at Staple Inn and had been working all winter on his version of Palingenius (see *Zodiake*, 1560, sigs. °2–°2v). He had, perhaps due to the death of his father, left Cambridge at some previous date without taking a degree, joined the literary avant-garde that was flourishing at the Inns of Court and Chancery, and sought preferment under the new regime.

His interests went together nicely, for as his work on the *Zodiake of Life* was winning him the esteem of his fellow translators,[37] it also found him favor with Cecil. The 1561 edition of the first six books is addressed to the recently appointed Master of Wards, and help with his wardship was only one of several ways in which the queen's secretary and member of the Privy Council would reward him before 1565, when Googe acknowledged "The fauorable accepting of my simple trauayles lately dedicated vnto your honor" (*Zodiake*, 1565, sig. °6).

Cecil was doubtless responsible for having Googe sent on an embassade to Spain with his friend Sir Thomas Challoner in the fall of 1561.[38] The trip proved literarily fruitful, occasioning a number of Googe's best short poems and exposing him to the works of Spanish writers that he introduced into England. Fifteen years later, Googe still recalled "the painefull passage of the *Piremies* [sic]" and "y° skilfull diligence" of one Henry King, who brought Challoner's horses safely through to Spain (*Husbandry*, sig. Q2). He stayed in Madrid until May 1562, when he traveled to Bilbao with a letter from the ambassador to his agent there introducing Googe as Cecil's kinsman and requesting that he be entertained at Challoner's expense and placed on the first good ship for England. One left on June 1, and presumably Googe arrived home shortly thereafter.[39]

The date of his return is a matter of some interest with regard to the publication of his *Eglogs, Epytaphes, and Sonettes* (1563). The book was entered to Raufe Newbery in the Stationers' Register during the winter of 1562–63[40] and printed March 15, 1563. In a prefatory letter dated May 27, 1562, however, one L. Blundeston explains that, since Googe left his poems with him while out of the country, he is publishing them without their author's knowledge or consent. In his own dedication to William Lovelace, Reader of Gray's Inn, Googe uses this circumstance as an excuse for allowing "these tryfles of mine to cōe to light." Although "a greate nombre of my famyliar acquaintaunce" had urged him to print his poems, he steadfastly refused until, as a result of Blundeston's meddling, things had proceeded so far, "& Paper prouyded for the Impression therof: It coulde not withoute great hynderaunce of the poore Printer be nowe reuoked" (pp. 9, 11–12).

It is possible to doubt Googe's veracity, since a ruse to secure publication for his poems while insisting on a gentlemanly preference for private circulation would not have been unique.[41] Not all the poems in the collection, at any rate, were placed in the printer's hands before Googe's return. Although he only admits completing his unfinished "Cupido Conquered," both "To the Tune of Appelles" and large sections of the "Eglogs" contain imitations of Spanish material;[42] and "At Bonyuall in Fraunce" and "Commynge home warde out of Spayne" must have been composed abroad. That Googe would take such trouble to augment a manuscript whose publication he claimed to oppose may seem less paradoxical if it is remembered that his was the first collection of short poems by a living author to be printed in Elizabethan England. Though he set a precedent many followed, Googe had to retain some vestiges of the established custom of unsought and unauthorized publication with which he was breaking.

After bringing out his poems, Googe became embroiled in difficulties surrounding his engagement to Mary Darrell of Scotney in Kent.[43] Letters compiled in Arber's introduction spell out in lively detail the conflicting claims of Googe and Sampson Lennard, the son of a wealthy neighbor of the Darrells, for Mary's hand. The efforts of Mary's parents to supersede their daughter's commitment to Googe went so far as to coerce her into signing a letter to him, full of allusions to filial duty, breaking off relations. The impasse was resolved by Cecil, who pressured Lennard's father into resigning the cause and referred the dispute to Archbishop Parker, who interviewed Mary, sequestered her from her parents, and settled the case *"plane et summarie,"* to

spare Googe a costly battle in court.[44] The story is one of families dealing for gain with their offspring and of Googe's bringing to bear superior influence to crush "the martiall furniture yat hath benne prepared
ageynst me, and ye Italyon inuentyons yat haue binne menaced
towardes me,"[45] but its elements of romance, crowned by the marriage
of the lovers on February 5, 1564, have raised it to the status of a local
legend.[46] The couple apparently took up residence in Kent, for the
births of several of their children are recorded in the Lamberhurst par-
ish register.[47]

Thus settled, Googe returned to his literary work and completed his
translation of Palingenius, which he dedicated to Cecil in 1565, com-
plaining of having had to work without "the familiar conference of
any studious frends" (*Zodiake*, 1565, sig. (‡)1). Next, apparently now
on good terms with at least the younger generation of Darrells,[48] he set
out to write something for his "verie good Sisters" Phillyp and
Fraunces. His satire called "the counterfeyt Christian" was destroyed
when nearly complete, so he dedicated to them instead *A newe Booke
called the Shippe of safegarde*[49] on Valentine's Day, 1569.

The prefatory material in the 1565 *Zodiake* and Googe's description
of his lost satire both reflect an increasingly enthusiastic Protestantism
keyed to the evolving tensions between England and the Pope. In 1570,
when these tensions were at a peak, Googe published his translations
of an anti-Papist satire written in Latin verse by the German Thomas
Naogeorgus and, appended to fill space, part of the same author's treatise on the Protestant ministry.[50] *The Popish Kingdome* is an interesting and competent piece of work translated by a craftsman of verse at
the height of his powers and, if we may judge by his having dedicated
it to the queen herself, for once fully confident of the value of his
endeavors.

As the new decade began, Googe had reason to look forward to a
period of repose and continued success. Although still kept from his
lands in Lincolnshire by his "stepdame . . . Long withering out a young
man's revenue," he enjoyed the favor of Cecil, created Baron Burghley
in 1571, and he could regard with satisfaction the substantial products
of his literary efforts and of his marital alliance as well. In July 1572,
when the queen called on Burghley at Theobalds, Googe was prominent among the attendants,[51] and in October he was granted the
income and arrears from lands seized by the crown from the estate of
an ancestor of his wife.[52] In the same year, however, with the death of
his grandmother, Lady Hales, Googe's fortunes took a turn for the

worse, and until 1585 Googe had to struggle to support himself, to educate his numerous children, and to secure his position in the world. He served Burghley and the queen at home and in Ireland, turned out a series of useful and improving translations, and did what he could by law and influence to get control of his patrimony and keep his social standing intact.

Between his six-month stay in Ireland ending in July 1574 and his second excursion, 1582–1585, Googe resided at Kingston-upon-Hull in Kent and interested himself in the pursuits of a country gentleman. Although he did frequent the court and Burghley's manor,[53] his most important work was literary. First, he revised his translation of the *Zodiake of Life* and in 1576 republished it in a form suitable for use as a schoolbook and compendium of knowledge. In 1577, he translated a poem on remedies for the gout and Heresbach's *Husbandry*, to which he added material of his own on curative herbs. The first of these is dedicated in familiar terms to the queen's physician, Richard Masters, the second to Sir William Fitzwilliams, whose service in Ireland Googe praises. Another military man he knew in Ireland provided the occasion for Googe's next publication, a learned epistle printed before Barnabe Riche's *Allarme to England* (1579), in which Googe firmly endorses his friend's call for the effective maintenance of a standing army. For his last translation of this epoch, Googe cast his mind back to his travels in Spain, and, brushing up his certainly rusty Castilian, dedicated to Burghley in 1579 *The Prouerbes of the noble and woorthy souldier Sir Iames Lopez de Mendoza Marques of Santillana,* a poem of moral counsel with a learned gloss.[54] The fatherly wisdom of this work was no doubt as congenial to Googe as he knew it would be to his patron, but he could hardly have suspected that a few years later he would need to arm himself with the Marqués's philosophy against the unfortunate reverses and entanglements of a second period of service in Ireland.

Googe's two Irish expeditions, although they have little connection with his formal literary work, yielded a batch of letters of some historical and human interest.[55] They reveal a strait-laced scholar and poet driven by financial necessity to immerse himself in an uncongenial environment and striving to make the best of it. In 1573 the Earl of Essex set out to conquer Ulster, and early in 1574 Burghley sent Googe as an "intelligencer" to keep an eye on the campaign. Seasick on the voyage, he suffered from dysentery for several months until recovering his health, he says, by drinking water from a rusty helmet. His outraged account of some untrained conscripts who resisted the officers' best efforts to make soldiers of them predicates Googe's advocacy of a standing army. Googe returned to England, commended by Essex for his abilities and uncomplaining service, in July 1574. Eight years later, in August 1582, he resorted to Ireland again, hoping to find "some abatement of my charges" while awaiting his patrimony.[56] Preferred by Cecil to Sir Nicholas Malbie, Lord President of Connaught, Googe was given the office of Provost Marshall of the Presidency Court of Connaught, a job combining the duties of quartermaster and prison warden. His letters to Burghley now combine pleas for further perquisites with gloomy descriptions of his life and the conditions of Ireland. Dublin is suffering from famine and the plague; the Irish even of the Pale are devoid of reason and religion, and Googe likens the feuding barons to "Eteocles and Polynces [*sic*] in Thebes" (p. 242). "The deddly fflux" is raging; Googe trusts he will escape it, although "I was never moar affrayd off my skoolmaster than I am off itt" (p. 242). Ever solicitous of his patron, Googe brought suit against a man who he claimed had slandered Burghley, and in hopes of adding to his meager income, he went to court seeking the post of Jailer of Galway.[57] In September 1583, he returned to England temporarily, and while he was there his stepmother died. In less than a year, however, he was back in Ireland, his Lincolnshire inheritance unsurveyed and his "poor wyff a dyscomfforted stranger in a strange Contrey" (p. 302). After having "to moyl amonge the Boggs" (p. 302) for another six months, Googe finally obtained the royal patent he needed to sell his office. The country had been pacified to his satisfaction, and, his financial independence at last secured, he came home for good in April 1585.

Googe seems to have spent the remainder of his life in retirement on his estates in Lincolnshire. In 1587 he was at court in June, writing a letter from Burghley's chamber,[58] and at home in Alvingham in August, dedicating to "my especiall good friends" the queen's physicians his prose translation of *The Wonderfull and strange effect and vertues of a new Terra Sigillata lately found out in Germanie*, by Andreas Bertholdus.[59] This pamphlet is the last work Googe published and, so far as can be determined, his last piece of writing to have survived.[60] Although his enthusiasm for the drug is naive and his style is flat, Googe pursues with undiminished earnestness his usual aim of helping those of his countrymen unskilled in Latin to the benefits they would otherwise miss. He died, perhaps of the plague, at Alvingham in February 1594, leaving his wife, eight children, and a shelf of books most of which had already slipped into oblivion, washed away by the tide of new works being written in England during the last decades of Elizabeth's reign.

III   A Note on Verse and Diction

The *Foure Bookes of Husbandry* was the most durable of Googe's efforts—in part, perhaps, because he wrote it in prose. Early Elizabethan poetry sounded laughably primitive in the age of Sidney, Shakespeare, Donne, and Jonson, and its verse and diction still remain the greatest obstacles to the appreciation of Googe and his contemporaries. The poulter's measure and fourteener couplets favored in the 1560s and 1570s have struck the ears of most critics as jog-trot doggerel, beginning with Warton, who held that "this metre of Sternhold and Hopkins impoverished three parts of the poetry of Queen Elizabeth's reign."[61] Because of the large type and narrow pages in use during the 1560s, most of Googe's fourteeners were printed broken after the fourth foot, which happily charges the caesura with the force of a line ending and eliminates the tendency of the long lines to sag in the middle.[62] Since Googe followed the principles Gascoigne would enunciate[63] of fitting light and heavy syllables into a rigidly conceived and continuously asserted prosodic matrix of alternating stresses, regular caesuras, and end-stopped lines, dividing his fourteener couplets or poulter's distichs automatically produced little epigrammatic *abcb* stanzas.[64] The effect is especially felicitous in short poems, where he strives for concision. Sometimes Googe breaks with the set norms, and the consequent rhythmic variations, because they are so rare, carry exceptional force. His use of spondees for emphasis struck Winters as an important anticipation of the strong and various rhythms attained by the later Elizabethans.[65]

In his deployment of the rhetorical figures whose presence indicated artfulness in early Elizabethan poetry[66] and in his adherence to given principles of decorum,[67] Googe remains, to be sure, a man of his time, but despite his artistic conservatism he is less imprisoned by convention than some. His elevated and figurative language seldom obscures the meaning it seeks to advance, and he can parody the kind that does. His base or rude style depends not on recherché archaism but on the sharp concretion of the spoken word. To a reader unfamiliar with the works of Grimald, Turbervile, Howell, or the translators of Seneca, Googe's poetry may sound primitive and quaint, but anyone inured to the endemic peculiarities of early Elizabethan style will hear a distinct, refreshing voice with something meaningful to say. In discussing the relationship of writers to established attitudes toward language and reality, Robert Pinsky has argued that "it takes considerable effort by a poet either to understand and apply those attitudes, for his own purposes, or to abandon them. The alternative to such effort," he goes on, "may be to lapse into mere mannerism or received ideas."[68] Although Googe certainly deals in received ideas, he understands them, possesses them, and, whether composing his own statements or, as in the work discussed in the next chapter, translating those of others, he applies them to real and vital concerns. His modes of expression rely heavily on his models in the rhetorics, the classics, and Tottel's *Miscellany*, but he escapes mannerism by firmly subjugating style to statement and cliché to the case at hand.

CHAPTER 2

The Zodiake of Life:
Epic, Satire, Schoolbook

BARNABE Googe began his literary career translating the *Zodiacus vitae* of Marcellus Palingenius Stellatus, and he returned to the task repeatedly throughout his life. Although the poem is unread and virtually unheard of today, in Elizabethan eyes it loomed as a major work, and the English version stood as the most significant accomplishment of its translator. Googe's *Zodiake*, in its evolution through five editions, its popularity, and the evident attractiveness to contemporary readers of its form and doctrine, constitutes a literary phenomenon whose nature and dimensions reveal much about Googe's career and intentions as a poet and the literary tenor of his times.[1]

I *The Decision for Palingenius*

Googe suggests why he chose to translate Palingenius and to publish his work in the amusing "Preface" mentioned above. Calliope, whom Googe elsewhere identified as "the worthiest sister among the muses,"[2] wins the day when she enlists him for her poet Palingenius. That twelve books of moral philosophy in hexameters, each named after one of the signs of the zodiac, should fall under the aegis of the epic Muse would not have seemed unnatural in an age that regarded Homer and Vergil as guides to life. In the dedication of the 1561 edition, Googe classes Palingenius with those bards, and the high seriousness of the epic genre pervades his version. "I could not," he explained in 1565, "(when I had long debated ye matter with my selfe) finde out a Poet more meete for the teaching of a Christian life."[3]

These considerations, along with the possibility that a respectable piece of literary work might open the door to patronage and preferment, emboldened the nineteen-year-old Googe to offer the first three books of Palingenius to the public. There were other incentives as well. In the dedicatory epistle of the 1560 edition, he mentions encouragement received from his prominent friends and relations, and surely the atmosphere of busy literary activity at the Inns of Court where he now resided contributed to his resolve to go forward with a project that was winning him the respect of his fellows.[4]

Googe could not indeed have chosen a likelier work to "english." The *Zodiacus vitae*, first printed in Venice in the early 1530s, was one of the most popular books of its era, praised widely and issued in over sixty editions before the end of the sixteenth century.[5] The poem was a standard grammar-school text and was even prescribed by law in some places.[6] As part of the school curriculum, the *Zodiacus vitae* offered clear advantages to the translator: an established reputation and an eager audience for the English version. Googe was not the only Englishman to attempt a translation; Sir Thomas Smith, as we learn in the dedication of the 1565 edition, had also "both eloquentely and excellently englished" three books, but Googe did not discover this until it was too late to abandon his own project.

As a piece of poetry the *Zodiacus vitae* is wildly various, ranging from elaborate visionary allegory to flat preaching and versified lists of information. Its encyclopedism helped to recommend the poem for use as a textbook—although it is not clear that Palingenius intended it as one. The student, at any rate, was introduced to a spectrum of literary styles, modes, and topics, and could find plenty of excerptable passages to copy out.

Although the *Zodiacus vitae* has been noted for certain idiosyncratic doctrines, the overwhelming majority of its teachings derive from that corpus of quasi-Platonic, orthodox, commonplace beliefs of the Middle Ages and the Renaissance now most conveniently referred to in E. M. W. Tillyard's phrase as "the Elizabethan world picture."[7] In Palingenius schoolboys found the familiar hierarchical creation with its plenitude of spiritual beings occupying a Ptolemaic cosmos at the sink and center of which stood man, prey to the insurgency of his lower faculties and diverted by the tempting dross of the material world from his proper quest for true happiness in the life to come. And they found likewise the Christian-stoic moral doctrines advanced since before the Middle Ages as the key to spiritual survival under such conditions of existence.

Of Marcellus Palingenius Stellatus himself little is known for certain. He lived from about 1502 to about 1543; the Italian version of his pen-name is an anagram of Pier Angelo Manzolli, of La Stellata, a village near Ferrara. It undoubtedly appealed to the English Protestants that the poet's body was exhumed and burnt by ecclesiastical authorities in 1549. To Googe it was evident that the Papists committed this outrage in revenge for Palingenius's having pointed out their sinfulness.[8]

Anti-Papist partisanship is gratified in several passages in the *Zodiake* that attack the corrupt Roman Catholic clergy. In "Leo," for example, Palingenius advises the prospective husband to make sure no friar, monk, or priest crosses his threshold. These "Wolues in felles [skins] of shepe" perpetrate all kinds of evil deeds "vnderneath religions cloke," "deflouring mayde & wyfe" and deluding the common people with superstitious fancies in order to take their money.[9] In "Capricornus," Pluto complains of the crowded conditions in Hades and wonders why God at least does not unburden it of His Own friars, priests, and monks. Later, the poet hears four diabolical spirits ridicule the Pope's plan to confute Luther with arms rather than doctrines, and there is just a hint that the Pope's doctrines alone might not succeed (1565, sig. PP3v; pp. 202–203).

Although Palingenius surely gained stature in England when his book was placed on the Index of Louvain in 1558, Googe's conviction of its utility to the commonwealth was grounded no less on social and moral than on sectarian concerns. In his letter to Lady Hales in 1560, Googe says he undertook his translation so "the common sort beyng ygnoraunt in the Latin myght receyue some profyte, and the longe consumed labours of paynefull Palingen myght be subiect to the vnderstandynge of the vnlearned people." The 1561 dedication to Cecil offers the *Zodiake* as a contribution to the stream of virtuous writings, "hole fountaynes" of which are required to extinguish the flame of "vice and euil life," and the new address to Cecil in 1565 expands on this idea, stressing the poem's moral value to a nation infected with vice.

Googe's translation, then, owed its popularity in part to the reformist flavor and moral beneficence of its source and in part to the intrinsic interest of its issues and information. It was surely also of direct and practical value to the grammar-school student reading the *Zodiacus* in Latin. A glance at the 1589 version of Vergil's *Bucolics* and *Georgics* by Abraham Fleming, however, reveals that Googe did not intend his *Zodiake* merely as a trot. Fleming praises Googe in verses appended to the 1576 and 1588 editions of the *Zodiake* for effecting the palingenesis of Palingenius, but he himself clearly had a different end in view for Vergil. He printed his unrhymed and dead literal text side by side with the Latin and bracketed all words not taken from the original, "considering," as he wrote in his preface, "the expositors drift to consist in deliuering a direct order of construction for the releefe of weake Grammatists, not in attempting by curious deuise and disposition, to content courtly Humanists. . . ."[10] Googe, on the other hand, although his work may indeed have relieved many a weak grammatist, *was* a courtly Humanist, and he held it as an article of faith that wide vernacular dissemination of the persuasions of a humanist education—in devise, disposition, *and doctrine*—could help to cure an ailing commonwealth.

II *The Evolution of the* Zodiake

Googe's serious attitude toward the translation—undoubtedly coupled with the hope known to all purveyors of textbooks for redoubled sales from each new edition—kept him at work on Palingenius off and on for most of his career. From 1560, when the *Zodiake* first appeared as a slim volume printed in split lines, to 1576, when it took on its definitive form in a handsomely printed 276-page octavo with index and marginal gloss, Googe worked over his text and made major changes both in the format and in the apparatus surrounding it. Typesetter's errors are corrected in the parts of the 1561 and 1565 editions that have been printed before, for example, and Googe welcomed the opportunity to make more thorough revisions for the entirely redesigned 1576 edition, which is advertised on its title page as "by him newly recognised." He admits, however, that he has been unable to polish it up to his satisfaction (sig. q2–q2v).

Changes from edition to edition in the annotations, prefatory matter, and even in the title itself reflect the evolution of Googe's attitude toward the work. The translator of *The First thre Bokes of the most christiā Poet Marcellus Palingenius, called the Zodyake of lyfe*, steps hesitantly before the reader as onto unknown and dangerous ground. The escutcheon of the "famous house of Googe"[11] is only the first in a series of shields behind which he takes shelter. Next comes the epistle to his grandmother, which confirms his aristocratic connections, claims approval from the prominent scholar John Bale, establishes his residence at Staple Inn, announces his unexceptionable intentions—to "dooe no less profyte to my countrey, then seruice to god"—and promises to complete the work if these "first frutes of my study" find a favorable reception. The fear that they will not is the concern of a florid Latin epistle in which Googe parries the anticipated blows of

"sycophants" and hypercritical "Zoili" and cites the precedent set by
former writers for composition in English verse. An acrostic Latin epigram on Googe's name by Gilbert Duke continues the attack on potential critics and prefers the matter of the *Zodiake* to the usual subjects
of epic poems. After all this fanfare, the well-intentioned young scholar
at last confronts us, with a self-deprecating shrug, in "The Preface"
and in "The Booke to the reader," a brief poem reasoning that, since
no one can escape "reproche at Momus hande," Googe can only beg
both learned and common readers to "beare the weaknes of my wyt,
/ and not thereat disdayne."

Such groveling would be as distasteful as it is insincere, were it not
for the ironic self-awareness evident in "The Preface" and further
developed in a jaunty ballad labeled "The Translatour to the Reader,"
printed at the end of the book. There are so many good poets now
writing in England, Googe declares, that Chaucer, Homer, Vergil, and
Ovid could all find an equal. What then will become of "this my
ryme," he inquires, and answers by calling himself "mate / Coequall"
to the legendary Cherill, a poet reputed to have written only seven
good verses out of a thousand and to have received a piece of gold for
each of the former and a box on the ear for each of the latter. Googe,
however, renounces any claim to be "Coparcener of his gayne" (sig.
H7v–H8).

Despite his avowed reticence and a level-headed sense of his limitations as a poet, Googe knew the value of what he had to offer his
reader. Nowhere does this appear more clearly than in the appendix
to the 1560 edition of the *Zodiake*, a manner of glossary saved from
pedantry by the literal-minded colloquialism of its entries. The flight
of Icarus and Daedalus ("a notable good Carpenter"), for instance, is
succinctly recalled but left unmoralized, and the entry euhemeristi-
cally concludes: "The verye trouthe was, he fyrste inuented sayles of
shyppes" (sig. H3v). A delicate restraint marks Googe's account of
"Ganymedes, . . . a boye of passyng beautie and feminine countenance,
taken vp into the skies by an Egle at Iupiters commaundement, and
made his butlar" (sig. H4). Both the wonder and the weariness experienced by a young student of the classics find expression: "Aetna, a
meruaylous hylle in Sicilie, continually bournying, named at this day
Monte Gibello"; "*Stygian* lake, a ryuer or lake in hell, by the whiche
the goddes always dydde sweare" (sigs. H3v, H7). On three occasions
Googe even breaks into verse. His versions of Martial's epigram on Phi-
lomela and some lines by Ovid on Tantalus are literal and compact.

An entry on Cybele with its rueful four-line soliloquy of Attis epitomizes Googe's usual way of treating classical lore. When her priest "*Atys*, a Phrygian," broke his vow of chastity, Cybele made him insane:

> In whyche fury, he gelded hym selfe with a flynte,
> addynge these woordes:
> > Lo here for my desartes,
> > With bloude I pay the payns:
> > O cursed bee the partes
> > That so prouoked my brayns.
> He was after transformed into a pine. (sig. H3)

Although the deeper mysteries of the myth escape Googe's grasp, he renders what he can with forthright efficiency. In his plain English, the passions of the gods and the horrors suffered by the mortals whose lives they touch are transformed into stark moral exempla in the same brisk, businesslike way that Attis is "transformed into a pine."

Despite the inclusion of three new books in the edition of 1561, the glossary contains only a few new entries at the end of some of the alphabetical sections. Most are of a factual nature, and Googe attempts no more epigrams. The tale of how Hipponax the poet gained revenge against the artist "Bubalus" for caricaturing him is included to explain an allusion in the dedicatory epistle. It reflects Googe's concern with the power of satire, for Hipponax "with Iambick verses soo vehementlye inueied against [Bupalus'] sonne that he caused him to hange him self" (sig. U1).

The text of *The firste syxe bokes of the mooste christian Poet Marcellus Palingenius, called the zodiake of life,*[12] follows the format of the 1560 edition, but its prefatory materials express the greater boldness of one who has already tried the waters of publication and found that he can float. Gone is the defensive weaponry of 1560—the coat of arms (it returns quartered with Mary Darrell's in 1565; Cecil's arms guard the version of 1576[13]) and the Latin epistle. Instead, a counteroffensive is mounted against the Momi and Zoili in a muster of Latin commendatory verses,[14] a dedication to Cecil, and a short letter "To the reader." In the last, Googe admits having been discouraged by his critics, but the "gentyll acceptyng of my symple doinges" by the public has given him the confidence to proceed. When he concludes by claiming the protection of two famous centers of the new learning and the reformed religion, Christ's College, Cambridge, and New College, Oxford, he is assuming an authoritative voice not evident in 1560. His dedication takes the form of a brief and self-assured defense of poetry for its power to expose and remedy the evils of the world: what vice or crime have poets "with sugred sentenses . . . not assaulted, with Godlye instruxtions battred, and thondring woordes exyled?" And what virtue have they not "hyghly commended, worthely extolled, and perfectlye taught?" Palingenius is a chief example, and his translator humbly follows in his path. The world portrayed in the first half of the *Zodiake* is exactly the diseased and degenerate one Googe sees as so much in need of the ministrations of his poet. A graceful woodcut of Adam and Eve being driven from paradise, which forms a particularly appropriate illustration for as much of the text as appeared in 1561, suggests the scale of effort required.

By 1565, when Googe published his completed version of the *Zodiake*, the satiric and sectarian concerns of 1561 had driven the merely pedagogical interests temporarily off the page. The newly elaborate title advises the reader what to expect: *The Zodiake of Life written by the Godly and zealous Poet Marcellus Pallingenius stellatus, wherein are conteyned twelue Bookes disclosing the haynous Crymes & wicked vices of our corrupt nature: And Plainlye declaring the pleasaunt and perfit pathway vnto eternall lyfe, besides a numbre of digressions both pleasaunt & profitable.*[15] The informative glossary has been abandoned, along with the comic and self-deprecating verses— these last presumably as beneath the dignity of an established courtier and diplomat, published poet, and married man. On the other hand, the clutch of Latin commendatory poems has grown, and there is even one in Greek.[16] In 1561 Googe could break off his defense of poetry in the epistle to Cecil to make a joke of his own verbosity: "your honor may iudge that through praising and commendyng of Poets I am rather entred into a Poets furye." In 1565 he is capable only of formulary self-effacement, and the defense of poetry, augmented by a list of poems in the Bible, a quotation from Vergil's "prophetic" fourth eclogue, and a celebration of English verse, now fills most of a long letter to the reader and spills over into a new dedication to Cecil. Palingenius is now described as a proto-Protestant martyrized for his satires on "the corrupte and vnchristian liues of the whole Colledge of contemptuous Cardinalles, the vngracious ouerseeings of bloudthyrsty Bishops, the Panchplying practises of pelting Priours, the manifold madnesse of mischieuous Monkes, wyth the filthy fraternitie of flattering Friers" (sigs. °7–°7v). The fervor of this outburst marks Googe's treatment of other topics as well. England needs the *Zodiake* to defend herself against infidels at home and enemies abroad.

Eleven years later, when Googe brought out the next edition of the *Zodiake*, a remarkable change had taken place. The satiric, anti-Papist aspects of the book are no longer touted as its selling points. The 1576 version and its 1588 reprint offer mainly information and enlightenment: *The Zodiake of life, written by the excellent and Christian Poet, Marcellus Palingenius Stellatus. Wherein are conteined twelue seuerall labours, painting out moste liuely, the whole compasse of the world, the reformation of manners, the miseries of mankinde, the pathway to vertue and vice, the eternitie of the Soule, the course of the Heauens, the mysteries of nature, and diuers other circūstances of great learning, and no lesse iudgement.*[17] A brief and restrained epistle to Cecil merely apologizes for the incomplete revision; all defenses of poetry and attacks on vice are omitted; and there are no further prefatory materials by Googe. Only some of the commendatory verses are retained; the new English epigram by Fleming concludes the text.

His recognition that his readers will use the *Zodiake* as a handy compendium of knowledge predicates Googe's main additions for 1576 as well. "For the Readers aduantage," as the title page announces, he provides an extensive, more or less alphabetical index locating discussions of such matters, to take a sequence at random, as "Precious stones, why they glister ... Path of vertue is narrowe ... Placed thinges followe the nature of their place ... Plotinus." This index has put modern scholars firmly in Googe's debt, but what must have earned him the undying gratitude of the schoolboys who used his translation as a study guide is the marginal gloss he spread liberally over practically every page. Many of the notes are explanatory, and occasionally Googe cites a source or directs the student to another work. Other entries mark points in the text or encapsulate an argument in aphorisms: "The hurt of wanton and lewde wryters" (p. 4); "Carpet Knihgts [*sic*] bred in peace" (p. 20); "The world a stage play" (p. 99). Googe carefully identifies technicalities of logic and rhetoric—"A similitude," "An argumēt, ab effectibus." Sometimes he intrudes a comment of his own: "The fond opinyon of Pythagoras which sauoreth of the musty leuen of Purgatory" (p. 104). When Palingenius speculates about the infinity of time and space, Googe remarks, "Friuoulous & vaine disputations" (p. 220), and when he advocates praying to the saints, Googe holds up a cautionary palm: "This doctrine would be read, but not folowed: for it is derogatorie to gods glory and maiestie" (p. 175).

The reader who approaches the *Zodiake* through the index or by scanning the gloss, as the reader of Rosemond Tuve's facsimile of the 1576 edition can hardly avoid doing, will feel himself dealing with an inert aggregation of information and doctrine, universal in range, but lacking a unity, structure, or dynamic of its own. A very different work emerges to the view of anyone determined enough to make a sustained perusal from "Aries" through "Pisces," especially if he uses the 1565 edition, with its large type and clean margins. Although Googe as the helpful, schoolmasterly commentator disappears, the poem that originally attracted his attention and that of his contemporaries as an epic and satire worth adding to the English library becomes more readily accessible. It is the shape and nature of that poem which will concern us next.

III   *Palingenius and the Humanist Dilemma*

Although its consistent moral purpose and predominantly satiric tone have not gone unnoticed, previous commentary on the *Zodiake* dwells mainly on its philosophical eclecticism and its looseness of form.[18] Tuve associates the poem with works in the tradition of medieval encyclopedic philosophical poetry and argues that it illustrates "that inter-dependence between Middle Ages and Renaissance which makes the two periods all but inextricable."[19] Although Francis R. Johnson is eager to find in "this most popular astronomical poem of the English Renaissance" some preparation for the Copernican cosmology whose growing acceptance he traces, he acknowledges its basically conventional vision of a hierarchical, geocentric, morally ordered universe. He nevertheless can make grist for his mill out of Palingenius's critical attitude toward Aristotle, for the work, despite its medieval flavor, partakes of the Renaissance ethos in respecting the power of human reason to understand this world and in being ready to discover truth wherever it happens to be found.[20] The following account of the poem will try to show that, in exploring the collision between the Renaissance humanist aspiration to understand and find happiness in this world on the one hand and the discouraging implications of the understanding eventually reached on the other, Palingenius endued his book with a unity of thought and structure that better justifies the esteem in which it was held than its supposed formlessness and diversity. The problem treated in the *Zodiake* was the central problem of life for the humanist-educated courtier of the sixteenth century, and the zodiac of topics and attitudes toward them through which the poem passes corresponds at least roughly to his passage from the enthusiastic determination of youth through the critical disillusionment of maturity to the abstraction and piety proper to an old age of contemplative retirement.[21]

Any argument for the poem's unity seems defeated at the very start in "Aries," when Palingenius announces that he will write "of much and diuers things."[22] But while he will sometimes be trying to reason out nature's secrets, for the most part, he declares, he will be pursuing those things that lead to a moral life (sig. A3v; p. 2). Lewd poetry is not one of these, of course, and suddenly, by way of an attack on vain writers, "Aries" becomes a humanist treatise on poetry and learning, complete with a reading list and instructions to the tutor. Virtue is impossible without learning, Palingenius concludes, and dedicates himself to composing a poem in which learning will be directed to the advancement of virtue. By far the briefest book in the *Zodiake*, "Aries" functions as an introduction. It begins with an invocation to all the Muses and ends, after proposing the subject and justifying the composition of the ensuing poem, with a few lines on the conceit of the zodiac that lends the work its external form and proclaims its encyclopedic scope.

The next book begins, however, not with an allusion to the sign of Taurus, but, more subtly, with a nautical metaphor linked to the appropriate season. The long winter is over and the poet may sail out on the seas of poetry once more. Since it is spring, the poet feels he should be up and doing—but doing what? Most men seek wealth, says Palingenius, which brings him around to the general subject of this book. Throughout the *Zodiake* the poet seeks to discover "What kinde of thing is blessed lyfe . . . / And how it may be got" (sig. B6; p. 10). "Taurus" argues that riches do not conduce to the good life, and a series of vivid set-pieces enforces the case. Palingenius deliciously catalogs a rich man's food, for example, then asks how anyone could eat it all without bursting his belly, and proceeds to describe in detail the nauseous results of surfeit. The wealthy man also experiences anxieties for fear of theft, betrayal, or misfortune. Virtue, on the other hand, which arises from the self-denial necessitated by "famous worthy pouertie" (sig. D3; p. 19), is proof against reverses. Contentment is available only to one capable of desiring no more than he can get.

"Taurus" rejects wealth and its pursuit in entirely pragmatic terms:

wealth actually does not bring the pleasure it promises, and one is simply better off poor. "Gemini" explores the relationship between pleasure and virtue in more theoretical terms. Its visionary machinery takes the argument out of the mouth of the poet, suggesting the revelation of wisdom of a higher order.

Walking along the shore one day, the poet meets Epicurus, a vivacious and rotund old man, who leads him under a shady elm to discourse on wisdom. To him it consists in knowing how to find "true felicity" (sig. E2; p. 24), or pleasure, which is the goal of all human endeavor, even of virtue. He takes Palingenius to "pleasures place" (sig. E7; p. 28), where the lady Voluptuousness resides in a lovely Arcadian grove. Personifications of various pleasures and their consequent pains march forth with her, followed by a rout of gods and heroes dancing with their heads enveloped in a foggy mist. Two monsters, later identified as Grief and Slander, bring up the rear. A beautiful lady in ragged clothes soon arrives with the warning that Voluptuousness is a temptress worse than Circe. As Epicurus scuttles off to join his friends, the poet sits down under a bay tree to hear the lady explain how man's reason should control his affections, but in the midst of interpreting the procession just viewed she is called away to heaven, because this sinful world is no place for Arete, the goddess of virtue.

"Gemini" demonstrates that pleasure cannot be reconciled to virtue. The allegory advances the argument effectively, and the sinfulness of Epicureanism is made explicit only after its consequences have been clearly imagined. So rich and significant did Palingenius consider his visions in "Gemini," in fact, that he continued to expound them in the next book through the mouth of Timalphes, Arete's son, sent in her stead to enlighten the poet.

The subject of "Cancer" is love, broadly conceived. Expatiating upon the figures of Venus and Cupid that attended Voluptuousness, Timalphes describes love as the creative and sustaining principle of the universe and a motion of the mind toward beauty. Friendship is a kind of love, and Timalphes takes the occasion to touch on all sorts of interpersonal relations and their pitfalls, enjoining the poet to deal with his appetites by finding a wife, to have good manners, to be a cautious friend to a few.

From neoplatonic philosophy to Polonian proverbs is a considerable drop. A more significant progression of tone and perspective takes place in "Cancer" as well. Palingenius begins the book with a invocation to Phoebus Apollo, a prayer that is actually answered by a voice from Delphos promising lasting fame for his poetry. Thus encouraged, he encounters, in a singing contest between two shepherds that he overhears, examples of poetic attitudes he should eschew. The first shepherd sings a love lament about the beautiful but disdainful boy Philetus, spreading the whole panoply of amatory topics and ending with a pledge of loyalty, however futile. The second shepherd deflates such ornate pretentiousness with burlesque. He describes a shepherdess so beautiful that a satyr is attracted to her and rapes her while her lover looks helplessly on:

> She cald, and shrikt, and I, as wood
>   would strayght her ayde haue borne,
> But sore afrayd I was to meete
>   the shagheard horsons horne. (sigs. H7–H7v; p. 45)

Now, he callously concludes, she is transformed into a shameless seductress, typical of all her treacherous sex. Suddenly, seven wolves descend upon the shepherds and their flocks, and the poet, after watching their struggle briefly, strolls away. The passions of these sin-hounded worldlings have nothing to offer him. A similar quick distancing concludes the book, when Timalphes remarks on how small the world looks from his vantage point in heaven and how silly it is for the inhabitants to be fighting one another.

Perhaps because it attempts to study with serious attention the human life just revealed to be "a staged comedie" for the amusement of the gods (sig. L7; p. 51), the next book is the least compelling in the *Zodiake*. No allegorical apparatus or fictional speakers appear to intrigue the reader, who must instead follow the poet through a tedious demonstration that, since only God is perfect, only He can experience perfect happiness. Man must be content with *relative* happiness, which inheres in the mean and sure estate, liberty, good health, and marriage. The discourse on the wedded life evokes practical advice on keeping a wife and childrearing (Palingenius favors strict discipline in both cases), and "Leo" dissolves in miscellany, ending with a lame pun on the "Lions tale" which is too long ("cauda meo prolixa Leoni est").

Man's triviality in face of the eternal comes into sharper focus in "Virgo." As if conscious of the flatness of "Leo," Palingenius begins by asserting that his poetry has greater value than the more entertaining but mendacious fables of the ancients. Calliope[23] now leads him to a stagy underworld where the Grim Reaper appears, "bloudy sithe in

hand" (sig. P7; p. 85), declaring that everybody dies and menacing the
poet himself. Removing the frightened Palingenius to more pleasant
surroundings, the Muse sets out to explain why he should not be afraid
of death. "Mortall state," she begins, "is nothing else / but blathers full
of winde" (sig. Q3v; p. 88), kicked about the rolling world by blind
fortune. Informed that she need not bother with riches and pleasure,
Calliope debunks nobility for the remainder of the book. Even true
nobility, which is the honor of virtue and personal achievement, not
the fruit of wealth or ancestry, brings no certain reward in this life.

"Virgo" thus follows in the *Zodiake's* progression of topics from
wealth to pleasure to love to the highest worldly attainment. At the
same time, it drastically revises the notion that the world may offer a
field for the accomplishment of worthy objectives. "Leo" proved that
perfect temporal happiness is impossible, but suggested the nature of
a relatively superior way of life; "Virgo" argues that this world in fact
has nothing to offer that we should not be happy to lose. Palingenius's
humanist aspirations, however, still not entirely extinguished, shine
through the seams of his gloomy logic. As always, he is most animated
by ethical topics, especially satire on abuses, and though Calliope
reveals that the true test of poetry is not vain fame in this world but
the judgment of Jove, Palingenius has his Muse crown him with laurel—"refusyng I"—before she flies off to heaven at the end.

To start the second half of the poem in "Libra," the poet mounts
with her to talk of heavenly things: the nature of God, the existence of
angels, the structure and operation of the soul, and its immortality.
Except for an artful opening and closing, "Libra" is a tedious presentation of orthodox theology and psychology. Twice the poet looks
ahead to "Scorpius," where he will trace man's destiny as an inhabitant
of what he speculates to be a darkened star ruled by the fallen angel
Pluto, or Sarcotheus, as he is later called.

"Scorpius" regards the earth and its inhabitants from the heavenly
perspective established in the previous book. The universe is ruled by
God's immutable Providence, but the sublunary world is ordered by
Sarcotheus according to his nature, which, being far down the chain of
causes and effects, differs widely from God's. Man's fate, insofar as it
involves material well-being of any kind, is entirely subject to the
whims of this god of the flesh. The virtuous man, however, does not
allow his affections to drag him into sinful desires for worldly weal, but
follows reason and shines the brighter for the material adversity he
suffers. Philosophically, then, the material world is for Palingenius

entirely fallen, and only spiritual goods are of any value. But the abuses of worldlings arouse his satiric ire or (at the end) elegiac sadness, and he promises to continue his portrayal of man's life with a survey of human foibles and sins.

Haled off at the beginning of "Sagittarius" to the top of Mount Theorea, the poet experiences strengthened mental powers and rises to the moon. Here he meets Timalphes again, who shows him the judgment of souls. To explain the predominance of sinners, Timalphes unveils the earth to view, where Sarcotheus and four ugly assistants are enthroned, and describes their temptations and the Dantesque punishments in store for their victims. Then, after a catalog of sinners and a lecture on wisdom and virtue, "Sagittarius" breaks off, as Mercury arrives to tell Timalphes he is wanted by Jove to help decide whether to castrate certain fat and saucy monks and, on his way to take a message to Hell, drops off the poet at home.

"Capricornus" begins with the returning Mercury's description of the crowded conditions below, and Palingenius, unwilling to add to the congestion, seeks from his Muse a model of the wise and blessed man that he can emulate. The ensuing discourse sums up the injunctions to virtue and learning developed in the previous books and finds their culmination in the life of retirement and contemplation. A wise hermit tells the poet that the perfect life is built around the quest for heavenly bliss, while pursuit of even the highest earthly goods is contemptible by contrast. This teaching constitutes the goal of the poet's quest, but his satisfaction at having at last found true wisdom in the world is dealt a serious setback by the scornful laughter of those diabolical spirits whose remarks on the Pope have already been mentioned. No man is *wise*, they say, only somewhat less foolish than others. Depressed by this view of human life as a ridiculous wandering in darkness, the poet hangs up his harp in weariness, resolving to turn from man to the mysteries of nature and the sky in the remainder of the poem.

"Aquarius" sets out to disclose the face of Dame Nature, or the secrets of corporeal existence. Its Ptolemaic cosmos is completely filled between the *primum mobile* and the moon with crystalline spheres that slide soundlessly against each other. Palingenius lists planets and constellations, numbering the stars in each of the latter. Just as the earth and sea are populated, so the heavens, far more desirable mansions, are fully inhabited by beings whose bodily substance is so refined that they can pass through the diamantine firmament like fish through water. The sublunary world merits less attention than the sky, but the movements of water and wind and other phenomena such as darkness, the seasons, and earthquakes attest to the power and majesty of God. Thus, though "Aquarius" lacks the explicit ethical concern of the previous ten books, its vision substantiates their doctrines. The earth is the dung-filled stable of the universe, while the sky, seat of astral influences and home of vast populations of angels, is clearly the most important thing in nature.

"Pisces," the last book of the *Zodiake*, balances "Aquarius" by turning to incorporeal existence. Repudiating his merely poetical Muses, Palingenius prays to God for inspiration. What he receives is the idea of an infinite universe of light beyond the skies, where bodiless saints and angels rejoice in the beauty of Platonic forms and endlessly worship God. The suspicion that this concept may meet with a skeptical response returns the poet to his earlier vein of moral suasion, and, in a reprise of previous themes, he argues that salvation is possible through virtue. The highest earthly good, he decides, would be to achieve a level of spiritual refinement sufficient to experience contact with one of the angels from the realm of light, and "Pisces" ends the poem with a prayer for angelic bliss, the highest and only truly desirable state of being.

The foregoing summary barely samples the subjects treated in the *Zodiake*, but it suggests how tirelessly Palingenius returns to the development of his central thesis, reducing the universe to the order of his moral philosophy and adjusting his ethical thought in response to the universe he envisions. The first half of the poem sifts through the chaff of human life in search of a few grains of true happiness, arriving in the sixth book at a perception of the vanity of man's life and the universality of death. The second half of the poem propounds wisdom on the basis of theology. After man's spiritual nature and that of God is set forth, Palingenius descends to consider man's life in a world ruled by the devil, arriving at an ethics based on contemplative retirement and a metaphysics in which a morally vectored dualism pervades the structure of the universe at large.

Despite the thoroughly religious tenor of his teachings, Palingenius states his case mainly in secular terms. Although we hear much about angels and devils—both sometimes indistinguishable from pagan deities—the Holy Trinity, the Incarnation, and the Resurrection are nowhere mentioned. Men's souls may be saved, but not through Jesus Christ, as far as one can tell from Palingenius, who apparently considered it improper for a secular philosopher to touch these sacred doctrines and confined himself to neoplatonic formulations instead. As a result, the *Zodiacus vitae* and its English translation deftly fulfill a number of often seemingly contradictory Renaissance literary demands, fitting the variety of human experience into a coherent and meaningful pattern without diminishing its moral importance, reconciling philosophical ideas derived from the pagans with familiar Christian attitudes, and presenting the whole through the medium of the highest kind of poetry, complete with fascinating adornments, but in a manner proof against charges of idleness, lewdness, or lying.

IV *The* Zodiake *in English Literature*

Since so much of what the *Zodiake* had to offer was admirable in the eyes of its sixteenth-century readers, it should not surprise us to find evidence of its impact on subsequent writers. The respect for Googe's effort expressed by his fellow translators at the Inns of Court was echoed by more disinterested commentators such as Roger Ascham (1570), William Webbe (1586), and Francis Meres (1598).[24] Gabriel Harvey called the poem a "pregnant introduction into Astronomie, & both philosophies" and remarked that Thomas Digges had committed "Aquarius" to memory. Harvey also praised Googe's translation as one that did justice to the original.[25]

Most of Palingenius's ideas were so commonplace in Renaissance England that their analogues crop up everywhere,[26] and no case for influence can be made on the basis of casual repetition of truisms. There is, however, substantial evidence that no less significant a poet than Spenser made direct and repeated use of the *Zodiake*. Doctrines expounded in "Sagittarius" and "Pisces," for example, not only enter into the Mutability Cantos and the Garden of Adonis; they also, especially in the latter case, illuminate some of Spenser's obscurities.[27] Some of Spenser's theories of love have exact parallels in Timalphes' discourse in "Cancer."[28] Although Spenser was demonstrably familiar with other instances of the images and ideas he holds in common with Palingenius, Rosemond Tuve finds convincing indications, including abundant verbal parallels, that Googe's version of the *Zodiake* was echoing in his mind as he wrote.[29] As a morally intended, philosophical, visionary quasi-epic containing elements of allegory, mythography, and even narrative, the *Zodiake* undeniably constitutes part of the generic tradition out of which *The Faerie Queene* arises, however different its ultimate effect.[30] Whether Spenser recalled the *Zodiake* from his school days or had read it more recently, it seems to have left its traces on his thought and art.[31]

Another of the English grammar-school boys who most likely studied Palingenius was William Shakespeare. That he did so, comparing the Latin text with a copy of the 1576 edition of Googe's translation, has been stoutly maintained by John Erskine Hankins, who devotes most of his book on *Shakespeare's Derived Imagery* to parallels between the *Zodiake* and Shakespeare's works.[32] The young Shakespeare must surely have been impressed by such an extended and by contemporary standards such a competent piece of English verse, Hankins argues, even suggesting that Shakespeare "remembered it well and probably knew much of it by heart."[33] As with Spenser, most of the putative borrowings comprise familiar commonplaces, but Hankins rests his case for direct influence upon the number of analogous passages and parallel clusters and sequences of images he uncovers, including certain verbal echoes from the English version.[34] Hankins digs out from the poems and plays hundreds of instances in which Shakespeare seems to have drawn on his recollection of the *Zodiake*. The richest single mine proves to be *Hamlet*, where gems from the *Zodiake* turn up everywhere, from the fatherly platitudes of Polonius through Hamlet's third soliloquy to the graveyard scene.[35] Hamlet's response to the foul-smelling corpse of Polonius and his whimsical meditation about the food of worms, his view of the world as a rank, unweeded garden and his animosity toward flatterers, his melancholy disillusionment with worldly pomp, pride, and ambition—all are expressed in language and imagery used in connection with similar topics in the *Zodiake*.[36]

Quite apart from whether it can be proved that Shakespeare read the *Zodiake*, remembered it, and used it as a source, the parallels between Googe's rendition of Palingenius and Shakespeare's treatment of Hamlet's concerns have a significant interest. For Hamlet's dilemma as a cultivated young man with a humanist education who must set right a corrupt and corrupting world is quite similar to that of the poet in the *Zodiake*, who seeks to employ wisdom in the effort to accomplish something of value in the world. And it is also exactly the problem confronted by the young translator and his colleagues in their effort to cure the ills of English society by administering a liberal dose of learning in the vernacular. That both Hamlet and Palingenius end up dissolving their noble worldly ambitions in a compound of resignation, faith in Providence, and hope for the life to come corresponds to the course of Googe's career as he progressed from the optimism of his early prefaces through his discouraging struggles for preferment and survival in Ireland toward the retirement and literary silence of his last years. Although Googe intended his translation of Palingenius as a contribution to the moral weal of his country, the book asserts the futility of such an endeavor, offering the chance not even for a tragic victory like Hamlet's.[37]

V Schooling the Poet

If *The Zodiake of Life* had an influence on any English poet, it had an influence on Googe. Ideas analogous to those of Palingenius abound in his original works, as do cases of identical imagery and phraseology.[38] More interesting are the various literary modes and styles that Googe seems to have adapted from the Latin poem he labored over for so long. The satiric elements of the *Zodiake* were especially congenial.[39] In Palingenius he also found precedent for his use of visionary allegory, for turning the pastoral love lament against traditional poetic love, and for his various lyric meditations on the human condition and versified exhortations to virtue. Further, the theory of poetry Palingenius advances in "Aries" ratifies the principles asserted by Googe in 1561 and 1565 and predicates the consistent moral seriousness of his work.

But it was from the sheer practical experience of putting over nine thousand hexameters into English verse that Googe derived the greatest benefit from his work on the *Zodiake*. Palingenius's Latin is frequently concise and epigrammatic, especially by comparison with the expansive copiousness of style widely favored in the 1560s, and the discipline of translating it may have contributed to the compression of statement that distinguishes Googe's poetry from much verse of his day.[40] Although Googe never mastered the subtle ironic tonalities of the original, his efforts to duplicate its figurative and rhetorical effects led him to some fine passages.[41] The following couplet from "Virgo" is occasioned by the changing fortune of noble families:

> Which as it did in time encrease
> so time shall it decay
> For time doth here bring euery thing
> and time takes all away. (sig. R1; p. 91)

The insistent but syntactically unforced repetition of the word *time* was suggested to Googe by the lines he is translating:

> . . . quae tempore creuit
> Panlatim, sed post quoque tempore victa senescet.
> Omnia fert tempus, pariter rapit omnia tempus. (*Zodiacus*, p. 137)

His transmutation of the inverted repetitive figure in the Latin to a triple parallelism yoked by rhyme shows Googe's skill in adapting Palingenius's poetry to a very different form of verse. Googe frequently adds to the concretion and particularity of his original through colloquial diction. In the same discussion of noble families, for instance, when Palingenius lists many men, "omnes / De medio plebis geniti" (*Zodiacus*, p. 138), Googe gives their humble background in exact English terms: "all borne of franklynes lyne" (sig. R2; p. 92). In "Aquarius" Palingenius argues that the heavenly spheres make no music. The beautiful silence of their rotation, however, almost makes up for the loss:

> [The] outward partes
>   of Spheares are smoth alway:
> Whereby they swiftly passe about,
>   no roughnesse them doth stay,
> And easly thus with gentle touch
>   their neyghbours next are kyst,
> Wherfore there motion they do make
>   all silently and whyst. (sig. RR2; pp. 212–13)

The language of the last couplet does full justice to the more formal Latin:

> Et sua contactu molli consinia lambunt.
> Propter quod motum faciunt sine voce silentem. (*Zodiacus*, p. 311)

Googe is least successful in rendering Palingenius's logical disputations and practical counsel, which often tend toward repetition and banality. When the matter is satiric invective or vigorous action, however, Googe's fourteeners come to life with urgent, thumping rhythms or sneering tones of disdain.

In his original poetry Googe was freed from the constraints of translation and could develop his talent for forceful colloquialism into a distinctively dramatic personal style. The capacity for self-irony evident in "The Preface" to the *Zodiake* of 1560 and 1561—but naturally absent from the translated text—saved Googe, at least until he wrote

"The Ship of Safegarde" in 1569, from falling into the trap of opinion-ated preachiness set in his way by his (and Palingenius's) idea of the satiric and suasive purpose of poetry. As long as he avoided this pitfall, Googe could successfully apply poetic talents honed in producing the book that established his reputation among his contemporaries to the composition of the book for which he is mainly known today.

CHAPTER 3

Googe's Short Poems: From Schoolwork to a Personal Voice

GOOGE'S small collection of short poems[1] appeared six years after Tottel's *Miscellany* in *Eglogs, Epytaphes, and Sonettes* (1563), blazing a path for subsequent writers of "songs and sonnets," who filled the stationers' shops with their books.[2] But while Googe may thus be considered the leader of an early Elizabethan school of poetry, his distinctive accomplishment in the short poem differs significantly from that of his immediate successors, such as Turbervile and Howell. Especially attentive to the example of Wyatt's poems, Googe found ways to charge with immediacy and a sense of personal conviction the usually impersonal and "voiceless" verse exercises in rhetoric and good manners out of which the mid-Tudor short poem was mainly built.[3]

Disagreement among literary critics and historians about the evolution of the sixteenth-century lyric complicates the problem of defining Googe's position. The old view of an early flowering of poetic genius in Wyatt and Surrey followed by a barren interregnum before the advent of Spenser and Sidney skips over Googe and his contemporaries, implying that their work was of little value or interest and led nowhere. On the other hand, the attempt to view the poets of the 1560s and 1570s as pathfinders who prepared the way for the later Elizabethans, while at least providing them a niche in the grand scheme of things, stumbles on the drastic difference in effect between poems typical of the respective groups. Apparently the mid-century poets, rather than simply doing a poorer job than their successors, were in fact trying to do something else entirely. When C. S. Lewis discriminated between the "Drab" style dominant in Tudor poetry up to about 1580 and the "Golden" style of the later decades, he meant to take this difference of intention into account. He claimed to hold no prejudice against the "Drab," but his preference for the work of the "Golden" poets is clear.[4] To define Googe as successfully "Drab" would be for Lewis as much as to dismiss him.

48

One of the severest critics of Lewis's view of the sixteenth-century lyric was Yvor Winters, who had already proposed an alternative polarity with a contrary evaluative bias.[5] To Winters, Googe's short poems formed a link in the chain of the plain-style or native English lyric, which included works by Wyatt, Gascoigne, Ralegh, Nashe, and Greville and stood in contradistinction to the eloquent-style or Petrarchan tradition that flourished like an exotic plant in the hothouse of late Elizabethan court society. The most thorough redaction of this theory has been made by Douglas L. Peterson,[6] who argues that the greatest poems of the age turn the rich rhetorical and artistic resources of the eloquent tradition toward realizing intentions typical of the plain style—the emotionally charged statement of moral wisdom about the central problems of human experience. Peterson's approach enables him to sort Googe's poems into several categories of style and purpose, including several instances of "the successful fusion of the plain style and eloquent conventions," especially in his use of the "principles of order" derived from formal rhetoric.[7] To Peterson, the difference between the early and the late Elizabethan lyric is by no means the *volte-face* suggested by the terms "Drab" and "Golden." Rather, the later Elizabethans refined or pushed to excess the intentions and styles of their predecessors, while writing on a broader range of subjects. Peterson's theory more satisfactorily describes Googe's particular successes than it does the practice of mid-Tudor poets in general, the bulk of whose works continue to strike critics as radically different in style and intention from those of Sidney and his school.

In a paper read at the English Institute in 1969, G. K. Hunter proposed still another historical and stylistic categorization of the sixteenth-century lyric.[8] The poetry of the "drab" writers of the 1560s and 1570s was written expressly for publication by government officials and office-seekers who wished to project a learned, patriotic, and moralistic persona conscious of the "larger claims of society," and "stressing above all things the common lot that holds individual egotism in check."[9] Their style is naive and their poems take on significance by reference to given, external norms. The sophisticated poems of the "golden" writers of the later period, by contrast, attain "aesthetic autonomy": "the individual lyric has absorbed into itself the moral 'placing' of its own material."[10] Although judging by his career and his avowed poetic intentions Googe seems the perfect "drab" poet in Hunter's terms, Hunter finds it easier to make his case by reference to the works of Turbervile and Gascoigne. He is careful to stress that the convincing presence of an individual personality in a poem is not the criterion according to which it should be labeled drab or golden, naive or sophisticated. In the drab lyric, however, such a personality is simple, literal-minded, and seen primarily in his relation to larger impersonal verities that exist outside the poem, while in the golden lyric a sophisticated personality, aware of conflicts within himself and capable of presenting them in ambiguous and symbolic language, is typically on display. By this standard, as we shall see, Google is in some ways a more "golden" poet than might be expected.

The following survey of his short poems shows how Google, by adopting a critical attitude toward conventional modes and themes or by grasping their inherent truth, broke free of the formulary anonymity characteristic of mid-century poetry and found himself creating unique and self-sustaining artifacts animated by a distinct and complex consciousness. The grouping of poems follows neither the undiscoverable chronology of composition nor (entirely) the order of the text, but rather is meant to reflect a scale of diminishing dependence on public resources—up to the last section, that is, which treats Google's confrontations with the problematical theme of love.

I   Rhetoric and Themes

Many of the qualities Hunter observes in early Elizabethan lyrics may be traced to the training in composition and rhetoric undergone by their authors in school.[11] Pursuant to humanist educational ideals, English schoolboys learned moral wisdom and good Latin by translating and imitating approved texts. With their handbooks of rhetoric open before them, they practiced the skills of expansion, compression, restatement, and paraphrase. They learned how to discover what to say on any topic and inscribe it in their commonplace books, and they learned how to arrange and ornament their compositions according to established principles. When they tried their hands at poetry in the vernacular, their works not surprisingly bore the stamp of their training, in style, structure, and intent.[12] Rhetoric is an inherently public mode of discourse, designed to convince an audience of the proposition at hand by relating it to generally accepted truths and values—hence the tendency of early Elizabethan poetry to refer to extrinsic contexts of meaning and judgment, hence its concretion and impersonality, its alternatively terse or copious style, its rigid, mnemonic prosody and verbal figures, its imagery of similitudes, proverbs, and analogies, and its frequently schoolmasterly tone. Tottel's *Miscellany* set a precedent for putting such exercises into print as English poetry, mixing them together as it did with courtly lyrics and old-fashioned didactic rhymes.

The mark of his schoolwork appears on all Googe's writings, but unlike many by his contemporaries, few of his poems give the impression of having been transcribed directly from his copy book. Although his pages contain epigrams imitated from the Latin and expansions of commonplace themes,[13] Googe rarely presents them unattached to some circumstance that gives them an aura of experiential reality. One instance when he does so is in "The vncertayntie of Lyfe,"[14] an expansion according to rhetorical principles[15] of a commonplace whose antiquity only serves to recommend it. Despite its solemn rhythms and a strong tactile image of life as the eel's tail "that harder held, / doth sooner slyde away," the poem remains a versified cliché: its doctrine seems stale and, if not untrue, of no particular urgency.[16] In Winters's terms, we could say that Googe failed to inspire a new recognition of the truth of the truism;[17] in Hunter's language, we could agree that, like the bulk of drab poetry, the poem does not validate its doctrine from within itself.

A remarkable effort to enforce this theme rhetorically is No. 174 in Tottel,[18] "Vpon consideracion of the state of this lyfe he wisheth death," which begins,

> The lenger lyfe, the more offence:
> The more offence, the greater payn:
> The greater payn, the lesse defence, . . .

and continues in the same fashion for eighteen more lines. Googe perceived the absurdity of the repeated *gradatio* and put it to use for ridicule in a poem whose title pretends that it is a sober expansion of a set theme: "*Oculi augent dolorem.*/ Out of syght, out of mynd." "The oftener sene, the more I lust," Googe begins, proceeding "lust . . . smart . . . smart . . . trust":

> The more I trust, the heauyer hart,
> The heuy hart, breedes myne vnrest,
> Thy absence therfore, lyke I best. (p. 123)

There are two more stanzas. A few years later the indefatigable Turbervile would bring the series full circle in "To Maister Googe his Sonet
out of sight out of thought" by at last uniting courtly matter with the
ornate device, employing the whole monotonous mechanism to assert
that he longs for his lady when they are apart.[19]

Although Turbervile missed the point, Googe's "clanging parody"[20]
demonstrates the potential silliness of substituting mere rhetoric for
thought and feeling in poetry. By combining a conventional theme
with an incongruous rhetorical figure in "Out of syght, out of mynd,"
Googe attains tension and wit. By similarly working two venerable
textbook themes against each other in "Of Money" (p. 128), he created
one of his most successful poems. Praised by Peterson for "the personal
conviction that comes through in its unrelieved severity of statement"[21]
and by Winters for its effective use of the spondee,[22] the poem is
equally notable for its original treatment of two opposed clichés. Out
of their collision emerges a new standard of valuation intrinsic to this
particular poem and expressed in the personality and tone of the
speaker:

> Gyue Money me, take / Frendshyp who so lyst,
> For Frends are gon / come once Aduersytie,
> When Money yet / remayneth safe in Chest,
> That quickely can the / bryng from myserye,
> Fayre face showe frendes, / when ryches do habounde,
> Come tyme of proofe, / farewell they must awaye,
> Beleue me well, / they are not to be founde.
> If God but sende / the once a lowrynge daye.
> Golde neuer starts / asyde, but in dystres,
> Fyndes wayes enoughe, / to ease thyne heuynes.

The praise of friendship was a standard theme set for rhetorical
expansion.[23] Numerous poems in the miscellanies of the period reveal
what sort of affirmation for this thesis could be gathered out of ancient
authors and commonplace books,[24] notably Grimald's "Of friendship"
(Tottel, No. 154), which Googe may have had in mind. Beginning with
the question, what gift of heaven is equal to a friend, Grimald rules
out health, wealth, and honor as temporary, demonstrates at length
that true friends never "swarue," and cites exemplary friendships from
classical times, noting that lack of friends, not lack of gold, is what
brings tyrants to grief.

Googe regards this idealism from the disillusioned perspective of an even more widespread commonplace[25] whose *locus classicus* is in Ovid (*Tristia*, I.ix.5–6): "Donec eris foelix, multos numerabis amicos, / Tempora si fuerint nubila, solus eris" (as long as you are well off, you count many friends; if times become cloudy, you are alone). The popularity of this idea may reflect its proverbial validity: "A freende is neuer knowne tyll a man haue neede / Nor then nother for any I know in deede."[26] Googe expands Ovid's theme, but by setting it up as a praise of money rather than a disprayse of fair-weather friends he enlivens the poem with irony and the conviction of having learned by experience natural to the proverb. Only a man in the heat of outrage, we realize, would so scandalously eulogize base coin.[27] The poet seems just to have come from a friend who has let him down; he even mocks his hurried good-bye in line six and, as Stephens remarks, portrays him hastily turning his back by contrast with gold, which "neuer starts / asyde."[28] The abrupt and acidic statement dissolves the cloying piety of such a poem as Grimald's or as Googe's obviously learned and rhetorically trained speaker might on wiser second thought have substituted for his delightfully bitter outburst. Thus with Turbervile, who, uncomfortable with the rejection of conventional attitudes, restates, expands, and reverses each of Googe's points, turning them into a tedious sequence of pious clichés ended and begun by the one phrase that reflects the immediacy of Googe's poem, the ironic address, "Friend *Googe*."[29] A less long-winded response comes from a poet of our own time, John Peck, who writes:

> Googe
> Is Scrooge.

II   *The Poetry of Praise*

An exercise whose popularity rivalled or surpassed that of developing set themes was to praise a famous personage, usually deceased. The handbooks provided detailed directions for this subtype of the *encomium,* including schemes for disposition and lists of the "places" of praise and, for the *epitaphs,* as they were called, the "places" of consolation.[30] Tottel's *Miscellany* again gave precedent for pursuing this exercise in English verse, and throughout the era the epitaph remained a flourishing strain of social poetry. The range of intention and achievement in the genre extends from the serious profundity of "Lycidas" to the hurried effusions of Elizabethan hacks who elegized recently departed notables and sold their poems as broadsides or pestered the bereaved families for patronage.[31] The form is plagued by endemic weaknesses: the incongruity of the subjects with the heroes and gods to whom they are being compared; the evident insincerity of the poet, who seems only too happy to have found an occasion to weep his floods of flowing brine in verse; and the failure of the prescribed turn to consolation at the end to carry any conviction or persuasive force.[32] Googe almost without exception avoids these problems.

His best is "An Epytaphe of the Death of Nicolas Grimaold" (p. 87). A natural consequence of ceremonial mourning is meditation on the inevitability of death. Following the precedent of several poems in Tottel's *Miscellany,* Googe draws together commonplace matter on the vanity of life and the universality of death and combines it with the expressions of praise for the decedent expected in an epitaph. He begins,

> Beholde this fle- / tyng world how al things fade
> Howe euery thyng / doth passe and weare awaye,
> Eche state of lyfe, / by comon course and trade,
> Abydes no tyme, / but hath a passyng daye.

The stately rhythm of these lines conveys the mood of wise resignation which the conventional elegy strives to attain as a conclusion. Googe, however, moves in the opposite direction. After a quatrain on death's destruction of life and youth, he narrows the focus to a specific outrage: "The gredye Grype, / doth no estate respect. . . ." As his diction drops toward the colloquial, suggesting immediate personal feeling, Googe asserts the human standards of valuation that death flouts but in terms of which Grimald will be praised. Rather than taking comfort from its even-handedness, Googe protests death's failure to make distinctions:

> Ne stayes he at, / the hie sharpe wytted sect.
> For yf that wytt, / or worthy Eloquens,
> Or learnyng deape, / could moue hym to forbeare,
> O *Grimaold* then, / thou hadste not yet gon hence
> But heare hadest sene, / full many an aged yeare.

If merit or virtue could escape death then Grimald would have. This consideration brings into clear focus what has been lost—Minerva herself weeps for Grimald, the Muses' flower. Another sudden drop in the level of diction and style now signals an outbreak of intense rage and frustration:

> A thousande doltysh / Geese we myght haue sparde,
> A thousande wytles / heads, death might haue found
> And taken them, / for whom no man had carde,
> And layde them lowe, / in deepe obliuious grounde,
> But Fortune fa- / uours Fooles as old men saye
> And lets them lyue, / and take[s] the wyse awaye.

The final couplet corresponds to one of the prescribed places of consolation—the worthiest are often taken before their time[33]—but Googe steadfastly refuses to be consoled; the proverb reinforces the previous expression of indignation. By setting up a scale of values between "the hie sharpe wytted sect" and the "doltysh Geese," Googe strives to insure that the reader will be as galled as he to find that Grimald's death can only charge the old saw, "fortune favors fools," with a new and painful immediacy.

That Grimald was a literary man like the poet deepens the sincerity of the epitaph, and Googe draws no satisfaction from the fact that Grimald's works survive him. Rather, what Grimald accomplished shows how little we can spare the works he now will never produce. A similar sense of a special loss in the death of a literary compatriot adds a nationalistic dimension to Googe's "Epytaphe of Maister Thomas Phayre" (p. 85). Although it was conventional to praise modern writers by comparing them to the ancients,[34] Googe converts the simple device into a complex conceit that structures the poem and expresses the animating ambitions of his literary generation. Phaer is to be praised for his translation of the *Aeneid*, so a comparison of his work with Vergil's suggests itself. Googe develops the parallel between Britain and Rome that is inherent in the comparison of Phaer to Vergil, producing a series of subsidiary relations that establishes Phaer in a position of superiority in England analogous to that of Vergil in Rome. Vergil's weighty style was the wonder of Rome, "but wonder more, maye Bryttayne great" at Phaer's success in finding such "swete accord" in the "barreyne" vernacular that "*Virgils* verse hath greater grace / in forrayne foote obtaynde, / Than in his own." Surrey, Gri-

mald, and Douglas did well, but Phaer surpassed them all, so that the
fates envied Britain and carried him off "in the mydst of all his toyle,"
leaving his "Worke vnperfyt so, / that neuer man shall ende." The
poem does not approach the resonance of the epitaph on Grimald, but,
by including a skillful argument for the cost of Phaer's death to the
nation at large, Googe validates the restrained emotion he expresses.

In a third poem celebrating a literary figure, Richard Edwards, who
died several years after it was published ("Of Edwardes of the Chappell," p. 97), Googe succeeds in making use of the stilted conventions
of praise by acknowledging how disproportionate they are to the real
dimensions of things. Spared having to contend with the solemnity of
a funeral, he builds into the poem a series of jokes based on the very
conceits he uses for the compliment. Asserting that Edwards may, with
the help of "Poets rage," be matched, but will never be surpassed, he
apostrophizes Plautus and Terence, previous masters of comic drama
whom Edwards deprives of what had heretofore seemed a similar priv-
ilege. "What wold you say / syrs," he inquires, "if you should beholde,
/ As I haue done / the doyngs of this man?" Surely they would be left
speechless and would "burne with teares" their mirthful books. At this
point Googe suddenly realizes that though Edwards drives the Romans
to silence, he himself is still running on, and abruptly bows out: "at thy
name / my muse amased stayes." By means of this foolery he manages
to avoid insulting the playwright by praising him in inflated clichés.
The net effect of bluntly humanizing the literary demigods Plautus
and Terence is to convey an accurate and reasonable admiration for
Edwards.[35]

Two poems in Googe's section labelled "Epytaphes" bear little relation to the ceremonial, rhetorical, solemn, and occasional genre of personal elegy athwart which we have seen Googe working in the poems
so far discussed.[36] That he so classifies them may reflect the influence
of Grimald's poetry as it appears in Tottel's *Miscellany*. Immediately
following a series of Grimald's conventional epitaphs are printed two
translated excerpts that narrate in experimental blank verse the heroic
deaths of their subjects (Nos. 165, 166). Googe, apparently misled by
their contiguity with Grimald's true epitaphs and by the incidental
passages of praise and lamentation that they naturally contain, took
them as precedent for two epitaphs of his own. "An Epytaphe of M.
Shelley slayne at Musselbrowghe" (p. 83) recalls the Anglo-Saxon bat-
tlepieces in its circumstantial description of epic conflict.[37] Here Googe
again reveals his sharp observation of detail and his skill in narrating

vigorous action. In "An Epytaphe of the Lorde Sheffeldes death" (p. 81), he does not rest merely with a tale. Including his name in the last line, he swears that he would have risked his own life, had he been on the scene, to save Sheffeld's. But the dominant emotion is neither personal grief nor admiration: like the epitaph on Grimald, the poem is animated by a sense of indignation at the outrage of order and degree. The noble Sheffeld has been killed by a common foot soldier, a peasant, a revolutionary,[38] a circumstance that substantiates Googe's somewhat overstated protestations of resentment, animosity, and dismay.

Most of Googe's eulogies, no less than "Of Money" or "Out of syght, out of mynd," approach the themes and modes of rhetorically based poetry from perspectives that put the conventions to more than formulary use. By setting one commonplace against another, by intruding everyday language and concerns into highstyle contexts, or by placing his material in a special frame of reference, Googe sets up conflicts and tensions that lend the poems a three-dimensional presence. Within that deepening space the reader encounters a speaker whose voice suggests a distinct personality, no matter how ordinary his opinions may finally turn out to be. In the next two groups of poems to be discussed, something like this process is inherent in the form, so that the interior dramatic space may rest on firmer groundings.

III   *Reply Poems and Epistles*

The ceremonious poetical game in which one writer makes a statement on some topic addressed to a friend who replies in kind was widely practiced in the mid-Tudor period, in school and out, in Latin and in English.[39] Although it offers opportunities for wit and irony, the dramatic potential of this versified debating too often went unrealized. The delight of the poems derives rather from the poets' ingenuity in adducing appropriate arguments to the topic or in capping one another's logic.

Googe's collection contains five sets of such paired poems—exchanges with his friend Blundeston and his cousin Alexander Neville—and four of Googe's poems receive replies in Turbervile's collection of 1567. In one of several exchanges on amatory topics, Googe successfully personalizes Neville, when, after a long discourse grounded in the usual piscatorial conceit on the dangers of beauty, he concludes:

> *Neuell* to the, / that louest their wanton lookes,
> Feade on the bayte, / but yet beware the Hookes. (p. 100)

Neville replies in melodramatic tones that the man who is able to feed on such baits "and yet to shun, / The priuy lurkying hookes" of passion is "A *Phoenix* ryght on yearth (no doubte) / A Byrde full rare to see." But whatever jocular banter may have passed between Googe and Neville on their experience with beauty's baits, what appears in the poems is mostly abstract received doctrine. This and the other exchanges, despite their piquancy, remain consistent with Hunter's idea of typical "drab" poetry.

The same can be said of Googe's address "To M. Henrye Cobham of the most blessed state of Lyfe" (p. 104), which expounds the ancient epistolary theme of the superiority of the country to the city. Googe was no doubt inspired by Wyatt's epistles to John Poins and Sir Francis Bryan in Tottel (Nos. 124–26), but while Bryan "trottes still vp and downe" or Wyatt reads and rhymes in Kent and Christendom, Googe and Cobham are nowhere in view. The poem proceeds in the manner of the first half of a disputation of thesis and reply and remains entirely a rhetorical exercise.

Rhetorical procedures need not reduce a poem to pointlessness, of course. In his two best epistles, techniques adopted from the handbooks provide a way in which Googe, like Wyatt, can effectively perform the function of the humanist writer—"to counsaile man the right."[40]

"To M. Edwarde Cobham" (p. 92) is a letter of advice to Henry Cobham's younger brother. It falls into two sections, the first of which is comparable to the first three parts of the exercise *chria*, a disquisition on a saying or deed of a famous person, as Richard Rainolde sets them forth: "Firste, you shall praise the aucthour, who wrote the sentence. . . . Then in the seconde place, expounde the meanyng of the aucthour in that saying. Then shewe the cause, why he spake this sentence."[41] Googe begins praising "Olde *Socrates*, / whose wysdome dyd excell," and states the sentence: he desired every youth often "hym selfe in Glasse to vew." Expounding the author's meaning, Googe assures Cobham that Socrates did not mean for the youth to delight in his "forme of fadyng hew," but to add "beautie of the mynde" to "the beautie he doth se," in order to attain a just reputation for virtue, "That flyes with fame, / whan fyckle forme doth fayle." The remainder of the poem takes the *chria* as an occasion for a kind of oration called by Wilson "Praisyng a man, the rather to encourage him": "In praisyng a man, we shal exhorte hym to go forwarde, ... requiryng hym to make this [*sic*] ende aunswereable to his mooste worthie begynnynges, that he may ende with honour, whiche hath so long continued in suche renowme."[42] Googe fuses the two rhetorical procedures by developing the idea of the mirror. After describing Socrates' advice on how to use the mirror to "know thyself" and then to act upon that knowledge, he puts the concept to work for Cobham, presenting in "My wordes a Glasse / for the to looke vpon." In the lines that follow, Googe reflects all the excellence and "towardenes" of young Cobham, in general terms first, then in specific praises of his mind, descent, courtesy, grace, wit, and, climactically, his good behavior, the sum of all his other virtues. Googe maintains the parallel between Socrates' mirror and his own by substituting for pagan fame the Christian glory of reward after death. Making a transition from thanking God for His gifts to the exhortation to requite Him, he then suggests that the "greater thyngs" foreshadowed by Cobham's "towardenes" can be accomplished through service to God. Finally, he confutes what "noughtye men" may say to the contrary and summarizes the whole case in terms of a promise of success and bliss, in this world and the next.

Googe's epistle of praise "To Mayster Alexander Nowell" (p. 90) can be taken as a companion-piece to the poem to Edward Cobham. Some thirty years Googe's senior, Nowell was a noted Protestant divine, driven into exile under Queen Mary, and around the time the poem was written, appointed Dean of St. Paul's by Elizabeth. Googe addresses him, in what might be called an eighteen-line English sonnet,[43] as an exemplary product of learning and virtuous discipline. The first twelve lines are one long sentence, which Googe handles well in syntactical blocks corresponding to the quatrain divisions. The first quatrain states by reference to Minerva, Phoebus, and the Muses, that Nowell is successful in matters of wisdom, scholarship, and writing. The next quatrain advances the argument by focusing on his supreme achievement: Nowell worked "In sacred Scoles." The third quatrain explains why this endeavor is singled out and contains the central message of the poem. Nowell has learned to live well, so as "to please the immortall kyng." A new sentence occupies the next quatrain, which begins what in a sonnet would be called the sestet. Googe sharpens and redefines the poem's statement by considering alternate careers that might have been open to Nowell. He carefully controls his terms, talking only about the *rewards* of various careers, not confusing the issue by mentioning for example that arts create beauty or that physic cures the sick. On the contrary, arts bring promotions, "Lawe gyues the gayne, / and Physycke fyls the Purse." But it is only through Nowell's vocation that we "scape the Curse, / And haue the blys / of God, when we be gone." The yoking of *Curse* and *blys*, a rare figure with Googe, emphasizes the difference between Nowell's career and the others. The release after the delayed caesura following *God* makes this line seem to be the conclusion. The actual concluding couplet, thus intensified, returns from the discrimination of careers to the more fundamental distinction that underlies the poem:

> Is this but one- / ly Scriptures for to reade?
> No, no. Not talke, / but lyfe gyues this in deade.

It is not the mere study of religion that counts, but the virtuous life that can result from it.

The purpose of this address, like that to Edward Cobham, is to urge a life of service to God. Clearly the counsel of both poems is directed toward someone or anyone in Cobham's position. In one, Googe appeals directly to an epitome of his intended audience—a promising young man. In the other, he couches his message in the praise of a representative of what members of the audience might become. Both poems give advice of general application based on entirely public values, but their statements are rooted in the descriptions Googe supplies of his individual addressees, and their tone varies with the circumstances of the poet's relationship to each. Although no internal conflict within the speaker reaches the surface and although no self-discovery seems to be taking place, Googe has found in the quasi-dramatic situation of the epistle a way to ground the poems in an authentic communication from one distinct individual to another, something he does not attempt in "The vncertayntie of Lyfe" and does not achieve in "To M. Henrye Cobham."[44]

In "To Doctor Bale" (p. 91) Googe carries this development a step further and shows even more clearly his control of syntax, rhythm, and diction in pursuit of refinements of meaning. Again he employs a structure of quatrains and a couplet to lead his statement through its necessary stages to a conclusion, and again a classical text plays an important part, although this time it provides not a starting point for rhetorical elaboration but a final reversal that turns the poem from sympathetic chiding to warm praise. Stephens has shown how Googe's handling of rhythm from quatrain to quatrain powers a movement from "personal affection and respect" through urgent concern to a conclusion in "simultaneous wonder and resignation."[45] The poem does not list precepts on proper behavior for aging scholars but presents the speaker's sequence of reactions as he gropes for a precept adequate to the specific instance he confronts. Although he stands in awe of Bale's long labors, the speaker thinks "For aged men / vnfyt sure is suche paine," and he urges him to rest his pen. His conflicting feelings resolve themselves when he calls to mind the appropriate text, perhaps, as Stephens suggests, the very one Doctor Bale is reading, Cicero's *De Senectute:* "there is also the calm and serene old age of a life passed peacefully, simply, and gracefully. Such, we have heard, was Plato's who died at his desk in his 81st year . . .":

> But thou I thynke / Don Platoes part will playe
> With Booke in hand / to haue thy dyeng daye.[46]

In a sonnet "To George Holmeden of a ronnynge Heade" (p. 113), Googe discovers still another possible relationship between the versified precepts and the dawning awareness of complexity of feeling or thought in the versifier. He fills twelve lines with sober injunctions against garrulity, only to pull up short in the couplet:

> But what is this? / me thynkes I heare the say,
> Physition take, / thyne owne disease away.

Googe thus parodies a poem on the same subject in Tottel's *Miscellany* (No. 286, "That few wordes shew wisdome, and work much quiet"), which runs on in a disorganized way for thirty-six lines.[47] The tension powering Googe's poem pulls between the meaning of its precepts and the conventional modes of presentation. Although the characteristic moment of self-irony Googe gains with his conclusion in no way calls into question the validity of the doctrine expounded, that doctrine itself cannot properly be called the true subject of the poem, which is rather a dramatic exemplification of "practice what you preach."

In fact, "To George Holmeden"cannot be reduced to a stated theme at all. The more fully conventional wisdom comes into contact with specific occasions, the more Googe holds it in ironic suspension, modifying, qualifying, or parodying it in order to fit it to the case at hand. And the more he engages in this kind of mediation, the more that intellectual and emotional process becomes the real center of the poem he writes. Now a persona of no neglibible complexity of consciousness steps before us from behind the curtain of convention, moving and speaking on a stage whose time, place, and circumstances are established by the words he speaks, and whose poem proceeds entirely within a frame of values he invokes. These criteria are seldom as nearly aesthetic as in "To George Holmeden," and sophistication is seldom the first quality one would attribute to Googe's speaker: he usually remains too earnest to become a "golden" poet. But poems like "Of Money" and "To Doctor Bale" should pass muster as sufficiently unified and self-justifying artifacts in any company.

IV   Soliloquies

In four poems, Googe starts so deeply engaged in particular situations that he seems less to be adapting given wisdom to the problem at hand than to be discovering values on the spot. Differing from "To Doctor Bale" as soliloquy differs from normal dramatic speech, all these poems use apostrophe to explain the utterance that the reader overhears. In "Goyng towardes Spayne" (p. 129), Googe addresses the soil of Britain that he is leaving; in "Commynge home warde out of Spayne" (p. 132), the sea that he must cross; in "At Bonyuall in Fraunce" (p. 131), his lust; and in "To the Translation of Pallingen" (p. 114), his half-finished *chef-d'oeuvre*. The first three spring from his trip to France and Spain, and since that was part of what interrupted his labors on the *Zodiake*, the four are linked by occasion as well as by technique. The clear generic precedent is Wyatt's "Of his returne from Spaine" (Tottel, No. 121), which develops a comparison of the Tagus and the Thames into a patriotic longing for home.[48]

"Commynge home warde" expands only Wyatt's concluding prayer for fair weather. Googe tries to reproduce Wyatt's feelings without developing the contrast of countries that motivates them, relying instead on his control of rhythm and diction as he confronts the last obstacle to his return to England. Descending from a tumultuous picture of the "Ragyng Seas" that "beate the shores of Spayne" through the strained firmness of the command "Cease now thy rage, / and laye thyne Ire a syde" to the measured repose of a final invocation, Googe expresses the consummation of the homecoming for which he longs through a simple caesural variation:

> And thou that hast, / the gouer[n]aunce of all,
> O myghty God, / graunt Wether Wynd and Tyde,
> Tyll in my Coun- / treye Coast, our Anker fall.

This poem contains neither proof nor precept but aims only to convey the emotion of the present moment. The companion piece, "Goyng towardes Spayne," states its circumstances more fully. By balancing a patriotic celebration of the "Pleasaunt Ile" discovered by Brutus with a contrast between his own enthusiastic resolve "for knowledge sake / to cut the fomyng seas" and Brutus's sadness at being "driuen clean / frō out his Coūtrey groūd," Googe plausibly renders the conflicting feelings with which a young man might set out from home into the larger world.

"At Bonyuall in Fraunce" uses the immediacy of the soliloquy as an ironic pivot on which to turn the heightened diction of love poetry and the melodramatic dread of irrational passion that was stylish in the 1560s into a neat expression of the poet's sense of his own absurdity. "Fond affectyon" wounds his heart and breeds his "restles payne"; "When shall my force," he laments, "beate backe thy force agayne." A final inflation of diction occurs in the concluding couplet just as he recognizes that despite his exertions, he runs on a treadmill in trying to escape from his internal nemesis:

> Safe thynkyng I, / *Charibdis* Rage to flye,
> On Scylla Rocke, / in Bonyuall I dye.

All the intensity of the previous lines collapses comically into a helpless shrug. There is no doubt, however, of the sincerity of his regard for the power of lust.

The idea of that irresistible power plays a key role in one of Googe's most personal and effective works. The refinement and maturity of sentiment in "To the Translation of Pallingen" command respect for the poet, still in his early twenties, who could write it:

> The labour swete, / that I sustaynde in the,
> (O *Pallingen*) / when I tooke Pen in hande,
> Doth greue me now, / as ofte as I the se,
> But halfe hewd out, / before myne eyes to stande,
> For I must needes / (no helpe) a whyle go toyle,   5

In Studyes, that / no kynde of muse delyght.
And put my Plow, / in grosse vntylled soyle,
And labour thus, / with ouer weryed Spryght,
But yf that God, / do graunt me greater yeares,
And take me not / from hence, before my tyme,   10
The Muses nyne, / the pleasaunt synging feares
Shall so enflame / my mynde with lust to ryme,
That *Palingen* / I wyll not leaue the so,
But fynysh the / accordyng to my mynd.
And yf it be / my chaunce away to go,   15
Let some the ende, / that heare remayne behynde.

The problem that confronts Googe in this poem is how to keep his
lament at being forced to leave off his literary pursuits from sounding
like whining after lost fame and ease. To counterbalance this undesir-
able implication, he infuses the poem with a tone of deep respect for
Palingenius, partly by identifying the work with the man and partly
by returning in line thirteen to the direct apostrophe begun in line two.
Even though he spends most of the poem talking about himself, Googe
does not cast himself in the dominant role. We see him not self-impor-
tantly working over an inert Latin text but rather, like a good servant,
humbly setting about to free the living mind of Palingenius from the
shackles of a foreign tongue. The earnest concern conveyed by the near
spondee in the phrase, "But halfe hewd out," and the determination
expressed by the deliberate monosyllabic movement of the declaration,
"I wyll not leaue the so," complement the general tone of respect and
give it resonance. The daring metaphor in line twelve lends credibility
to the commitment Googe goes on to make: his mind is being inflamed
as lust inflames the body, but with the compulsion to versify instead of
animal desire. An overwhelming force like that of lust, but directed to
rational and praiseworthy ends, will bring him back to his neglected
task. The last two lines put his selfless dedication to Palingenius in
explicit terms. They might have seemed a perfunctory disclaimer were
it not that the attitude they express is discovered through or engen-
dered out of the careful refinements of feeling in the previous lines, so
that they ring with sincerity.

Googe never abandoned the idea that poetry should inculcate virtue;
neither was he often content merely to versify preformulated doctrine
in ready-made rhetorical modes and structures. Whether by noting
inconsistencies within the conventional materials, by testing them
against his experience of particular instances they should govern, or,

through parody, by gaining the ironic perspective that enabled him to see through and beyond them, he repeatedly turned his poems into acts of imaginative realization and discovery. The soliloquy poems, based on personal occasions that demand such realization and discovery, dispense with given precepts or else integrate them into the more complex awareness being attained.

Googe's dissatisfaction with formulary banality and his determination to cleave sincerely to the truth he was discovering about the subject matter of the poem at hand placed him in an awkward position when he confronted the most conventional and widely exploited sixteenth-century poetic tradition of all. His efforts to use for love the strategies that were so productive on non-amatory topics comprise a fascinating and unconventional collection of love (or *anti*love) poems.

V The Matter of Love

By far the greatest portion of *Eglogs, Epytaphes, and Sonettes* is devoted in one way or another to love. Amatory poetry dominated Tottel's *Miscellany;* indeed, love formed the principal theme of the short poem in England throughout the century. One ought, if one were writing poetry, to follow the example set by the ancients, the Italians, and the writers in Tottel and generations of courtly makers before them. But when Googe turned to love, he found his eagerness to follow literary tradition in serious conflict with his philosophical attitudes. The sensuality of the pagans and the postured sufferings of courtly and Petrarchist lovers appear both foolish and evil in the eyes of Christian stoicism. In trying to resolve this conflict, Googe, like many of his fellow Tudor poets, was brought face to face with fundamental questions not only about love but also about its favored vehicle of expression, poetry itself. Although he did not reach any positive synthesis comparable, say, to that of Spenser in *Epithalamion*, his struggles with the problem led him into new areas of poetic achievement. Here we will see how Googe coped with love in his short poems; in the next chapter we will trace his more thorough exploration of the topic in the "Eglogs" and "Cupido Conquered."

We have already seen Googe and Alexander Neville playing with the idea that female beauty is a baited hook which men, led astray by affection, bite to their pain, and we have seen Googe at Bonneville in France fleeing headlong before his passion. Another disputatious exchange puts the notion into its larger moral context. In "To L. Blundeston" (p. 99), Googe discriminates among various keys to wisdom, concluding that "the wysest wyght" is he "Whom God gyues grace / to rule affections ryght." Blundeston's answer fills in the canvas; affection stirs prideful ambition, shuns moderation, causes unfaithfulness, *and* breeds indiscreet love. Again, in "To Alexander Neuell of the blessed S[t]ate of him that feeles not the force of Cupids flames"(p. 107), Googe catalogs the conventions of poetic love to show why love should be avoided. These things belong in poetry, Googe seems to feel; he must use them, but his habitual categories of thought reveal them as at best absurd, but mainly as self-destructive and morally evil.

And Googe, unlike many poets,[49] usually refuses to leave the moral categories out of account in treating love. There is only one poem in his collection that calmly asserts the conventions of amatory complaint. This is "To the Tune of Appelles" (p. 137), and its unique character stems from its musical aims. Seeking to ground a simple message in easily grasped and emotionally charged terms, Googe took the conceits for his song from a shepherd's lament in Montemayor's *Diana*, where he found gathered together a remarkable number of amatory commonplaces.[50] All nature laments with the lover; the seasons change, but "Stil styl do rage my restles paynes"; he is enslaved; his "wyt" is "cōsumde w^t thought"; he shuns company. The lady's beauty is described in terms of "Golde ... Crystall ... Rubyes" and "Alablaster"; her heart is "of Flynt and Marble Stone." But like a true lover, the poet will not give over: "Let not thy Seruant dye for the," he pleads, and begs for favor still.

It is a tour de force, as if Googe wished by exhausting the amatory conventions in a single song to earn the antagonistic attitude he adopts toward them in other poems. This is surely the case in an untitled couplet that illustrates graphically how little substance actually fills the inflated stanzas of love poetry:

> Two Lynes shall tell the Gryefe
> that I by Loue sustayne.
> I burne, I flame, I faynt, I fryse,
> of Hell I feele the payne. (p. 124)

Turbervile in response naturally gave a two-line *Remedia Amoris*: "Let Reason rule where Loue did raigne, / and ydle thoughts eschewe."[51] Easier said than done within the tradition that credits love with instant and lasting sway over reason, but the ancient injunction forms the basis of Googe's program in love poetry, which is to gain a clear apprehension of the destructive passion and to free the poetic consciousness from its domination.

Some lines taken "Out of an olde Poet" (p. 119) provide Googe with a soliloquy similar to those discussed above that expresses the struggle of the rational will to resist the impulses of affection. Rather than committing "so foule an acte" as his lust drives him to, the speaker prefers that his "carryon vyle" be burned to dust or that the sickness of his fancy,

> O gapyng Hell, / dry[u]e me now downe to the,
> Let boylyng syghes, / consume me all to nought.[52]

The intensity generated by the heightened diction and the spondees in the next-to-last line reflects firm determination. The traditional force of the love-sufferings gives the self-contemptuous speaker an almost heroic stature in his willingness to bear them. We shall see how Googe developed the possibilities of such self-control in "To Maystresse A.," discussed below. But in three untitled poems immediately following "Out of an olde Poet" Googe explores the condition of the enamored mind in the popular Petrarchist terms.

One (p. 121) describes the effects on the poet of encountering his beloved. Hearing her name, he wishes to see her face, but seeing her causes his blood to boil and beat in his veins. When she speaks, he pales and blushes, and his mood is totally dependent on whether she smiles or frowns, but it is his fate "That I shuld burne & thou yet know, / no whytt of all my wo." The poem details the standard situation of courtly love—the habitual present tense asserts the eternal immutability of the love relationship as frozen in poetry. Like the racing men and maidens of Keats's urn, the lover is always straining, the beloved is never yielding. Googe renders not the beauty of the situation but its pain—pain redoubled by the frustration with which his poem comes to rest.

In the sonnet, "Vnhappye tonge, / why dydste thou not cōsent" (p. 122), the poet blames his tongue and heart for missing an opportunity of suit. The conceit is analogous to Wyatt's version of a poem by Petrarch (Tottel, No. 48, "Against his tong that failed to vtter his sutes"), but Googe develops it differently, severing himself from the tongue that would not speak but now complains, the heart that burns within but made no sign: their troubles are their own fault. Thus the poet, however sophistically, rises above the servile and suffering role

into which he is cast by amatory convention. The love and the suffering belong only to the body; the soul stands apart.

In "Ons musynge as I sat" (pp. 120, 174), Googe's speaker gains a
more honest detachment through the familiar emblem of the lover as
a moth attracted to a flame.[53] He watches a "symple selye Flye" flitting
about his candle. It seems carefree and happy, and he envies it, for,
without reason, it lives "voyde of woe." The ultimate fate of the moth
is well known, of course. Both the moth and the poet are behaving
stupidly, but the poet's reason, which should direct him away from the
dangerous flame, can serve in the case of love only to increase his suffering. He thinks he would like to change places with the moth: if he
must burn, he might as well be happy doing it. By portraying a man
whose reason love has subverted drawing false conclusions from the
image of himself in the moth, Googe constructs a double mirror that
reflects the true depth of love's destruction of the self.

In "The Harte absent" (p. 116), Googe splits his ironic awareness of
the folly of love into two voices. The lover begins, after the manner of
Wyatt in "Help me to seek,"[54] inquiring after his lost heart: "Swete
muse tell me, / wher is my hart becom." We may imagine this lan-
guishing lover to be quite surprised a few lines later to hear his Muse
answer in severe terms the merely rhetorical question he has put to
her. If he wants to know where his heart is, it is, "Sir Foole in place,
/ wher as it shuld not be / . . . And wher for thee," she concludes, "as
much be sure they passe: / As dyd the master, / ons for *Esops* Asse."
Here Googe again uses colloquial diction to measure a falsely elevated
posture, establishing for the Muse just the right tone of arch exaspera-
tion, which culminates in the apt allusion to Aesop.[55] She has been
exercised to the limit of her patience in these paltry love affairs.

Googe further develops this attitude toward poetic love in two
poems that employ mock-heroic strategies to satirize amatory overstatement. In a traditional Valentine game, the names of all the ladies
present were placed on scrolls, and each gentleman drew out by lot the
"mistress" he was to "serve" for the day.[56] When Googe comes up with
the wrong girl in "Of the vnfort[u]nate choyse of his Valentyne" (p.
124), he vents his spleen in one long sentence of imprecation, calling
down "The Paynes that all the Furyes fell / can cast frō Lymbo lake"
and a host of other tortures on "this cursed hand" that, when his mistress's name was still in the hopper, drew a stranger's, to "torment my
pauled Spryght." His playful overstatement of his disappointment parodies the specious inflation of amatory laments, specifically perhaps

that of Tottel No. 179, "Hell tormenteth not the damned ghostes so sore as vnkindness the louer." The playfulness does not sheathe the poem's cutting edge, which consists in a perception of identity between the self-important pomp of conventional poetic love and the trivial dalliance of court games.

In "To Maystresse D." (p. 118), Googe files his parodic blade into the point of a private joke. A haughty, nearly Vergilian rhythm, as Peterson points out,[57] and a series of mythological allusions associate the poem with the style of learned eloquence favored for ceremonial occasions. But Googe negates the mythology: his letter does *not* come from Venus' throne, and when he finally comes to the true source of his complaint, though he allows himself the apparent extravagance of calling absence from his mistress a "Dongeon deepe," it is *not* one ruled by Pluto or Proserpine. He writes out of "duetie" and good-natured wit: Mistress D. is his bride-to-be Mary Darrell, and "Dongeon" is the name of his grandmother's manor house near Canterbury, not far from the Darrells' seat at Scotney.

Like the Valentine poem, "To Maystresse D." strips the love conventions of their claim to express emotion by making fun of them. It also depends upon that humor to replace the putative emotion as the meaningful substance of the poem. Although Googe implies that something solid and true exists between himself and Mary by contrast with which the love conventions parodied seem to be inane, he makes no effort to say what it is. The only positive alternative for poetry that Googe could discover to the poetic love he repudiated was the moral philosophy that found it wanting.

Googe could hardly address Mary Darrell on the immorality of love while in the very process of wooing her, but he could berate a theoretical mistress in such terms. "To Maystresse A." (p. 109)—that is, anybody—begins as an ordinary love complaint but develops within its dramatic context the whole moral position against love and ends by telling the lady (literally) to go to hell. Although the lover has suffered long, the lady for some reason disregards one who values her so highly, "and next to God, / hath dearest in his brest." The poet's care to save a place for God is laden with implications.[58] By admitting the simultaneous existence of a higher principle than his love for his mistress, Googe breaks down the conventional separation between the laws of Love and the laws of Reason, suggesting that the lover must somehow obey them both at once. Continuing to parrot amatory lore, he works out an unusual syllogism. The lady is so cruel that she seems to have been "fostred in the Caues, / of Wolues or Lyons wylde." Why, then, did not God give her "a fowle yll fauerde face" to match her "Tygers Harte"? Surely because "he lykes no Louers trade" and has therefore clothed "a ragynge Fende" with "an Angels face." Out of the cruelty of the mistress emerges a recognition of the ungodliness of love. But instead of shrugging off love and bidding farewell to his lady, something the enamored lover, caught on the barbed hook of beauty, is not supposed to be able to do, Googe brings God's laws right into a situation that is still regulated and determined by the laws of Love. He has a better answer than the threat of suicide prescribed for his case by tradition. "Well now take this for ende of all," he says huffily, "I loue and thou doste hate," but "Paynes can not last for euermore" and in his old age he will be able to see the folly of his youth. By that time, he continues, her beauty will be gone and he will rejoice to be free at last from that which has enchained him. Meanwhile, he plans to "keepe close / my flames and let them blase" within, praying that he will live to "neglecte thy folysh face," and concluding, "God keepe thee far from me, / And sende thee in that place to dwell, / that I shall neuer see."

The idea recalls Wyatt's "My lute awake" (Tottel, No. 87), in which a cruel lady's ultimate decay is viewed with similar satisfaction by the poet. But Wyatt's lutanist sings with blithe irony and makes no pretense of suffering any longer—a tone Googe catches more closely in "A Refusall" (p. 127), discussed in the next chapter. Further, for Wyatt, the issue is one more of justice than of morality. In "To Maystresse A.," Googe's lover, by professing continued love even as he pronounces his *"Apage Satana,"* assumes a posture of heroic—and inevitably mock-heroic—suffering. In its self-contradictory extravagance of sentiment, the poem fails even as satire, since the poet is both victim as foolish lover and satirist in his awareness of his folly. His morally tough plan for escape, it turns out, is what is most laughable of all. Strung up between two conflicting theories, Googe is left in this poem dangling quite out of touch with the solid ground of real life on which he stands in "To Maystresse D." and the best of his nonamatory poems.

But it would be wrong to conclude that Googe was always defeated by the love convention. That he could turn out polished verse in standard amatory terminology is evident in "Of Maistres .DS." (p. 127), where he follows the pledge-of-service pattern and combines it with muted formulas of praise to produce an elegant compliment, charged with genuine respect.[59] Googe praises the lady's speech, modest appearance, and courtesy. These things have bound his heart to her, he concludes,

> In pledge wherof, / my seruyce here I gyue
> Yf thou so wylte, / to serue the whylst I lyue.

This poem is not confined by the conventions it employs. Googe's pledge is motivated not by Cupid's darts of blind affection but by a just and reasonable gratitude. The self-restraint implied by the quali- fication, "Yf thou so wylte," comes to life in the caesural pause that follows it, from which the conventionally phrased emotion flows away in the rest of the line smoothly and swiftly.

This dignified treatment of amatory material, like the use Googe makes of other conventions in such poems as those to Bale, on Grimald, and to Edward Cobham, contributes to his discovery and statement of the truth of the occasion at hand. But Googe was not content to ignore the infection of poetry by a kind of love he could not abide. In the "Eglogs" and "Cupido Conquered," as in a number of the short poems just discussed, he attacked poetic love as he understood it in its own terms and on its own ground.

Ironically, Googe's most successful short poems were just those that the taste of his generation regarded as least significant.[60] That Googe probably shared this judgment may explain why he wrote no lyrics after 1563. The frame of mind that took a vast, mostly uncritical com- pendium of commonplace doctrine such as the *Zodiake* as a major con- tribution to the moral weal of the nation would not be likely to place much value on the strained refinements of private consciousness in a poet trying to decide what to think of the death of a mentor, an aging friend's labors, or a conflict of duties. Although we may regret that Googe could not recognize what he had achieved in his short poems clearly enough to be inspired to write more, we may rest assured that he himself took great satisfaction from the public and utilitarian works to which he later turned. The "Eglogs" and "Cupido Conquered" in certain ways foreshadow Googe's subsequent development, and "The Ship of Safegarde" marks the point of no return. The first two evolve from the private and inward modes of eclogue and dream vision moral statements of public, though literary, application; the last, although privately addressed to his wife's sisters, is nothing more nor less than a public sermon, fit for any pulpit in the realm.

CHAPTER 4

Googe's Longer Poems: Eclogue, Allegory, Sermon

FROM Wyatt on, the efforts of Tudor writers to reconcile amatory poetic conventions with Christian-humanist moral philosophy made important contributions to the development of English poetry. Since ethical analysis invites a notation of causes and consequences in temporal sequence, the moral approach to love had often substituted retrospective repudiations for the endless stasis of the conventional complaint.[1] While such poems as Wyatt's "Farewell, Loue, and all thy lawes for euer" (Tottel, No. 99) or Donne's "Farewell to Love" must claim to be the *last* love poem, it is a short step from looking back over one's shoulder at former follies to setting them forth as admonitory bad examples. The idea occurred among others to Turbervile, who claimed that his book of love poetry was meant to "warne . . . all tender age to flee that fonde and filthie affection of poysoned & vnlawful loue,"[2] and it certainly had something to do with the birth of the English sonnet sequence.[3] Though Googe did not pursue this line of development, in "To Maystresse A." he showed that he could match its hindsight with a similarly diachronic awareness of future possibilities.

The idea that love relationships, albeit begun by Cupid's dart, are not eternally fixed but can end at the will of the lover led Googe to one brief "out-of-love"[4] poem comparable to some of Wyatt's brusque farewells: "Fortune fauoures not / and all thynges backward go," he says, so "Farewell I wast no vayner wordes, / I Hope for better day" (p. 127). But the simple immediacy of "A Refusall" confines any moral evaluation of the case to unanalyzable implications. We hear only one side of the story, and the choice made arises from pragmatic common sense rather than virtue.

A full investigation of the problem of poetic love required a more commodious genre. Googe turned not to the sequence of short poems but to the pastoral eclogue, the dream vision, and the quasi-allegorical homily in verse. Much more hospitable than the short poem or the

72

sonnet sequence to the discursive or symbolic treatment of ideas, these forms gave Googe a way to work the issue through.

It has been shown that genre was not a determining concern for mid-Tudor poets;[5] Googe, however, did know exactly what he meant by "eglog" or "dreame," and he exploited their special resources in his critique of literary love. Love is not the whole subject of "The Ship of Safegarde," but we shall see that Googe treats it there as part of his sermon on the voyage of the soul through the perilous seas of life in allegorical terms similar to those evolved for it in the "Eglogs" and "Cupido Conquered."

I The "Eglogs"

As the only original set of eclogues in English between Barclay[6] and Spenser, containing the first English use of passages from the *Diana* of Montemayor, Googe's pastoral sequence has long interested literary historians.[7] But the search for anticipations of *The Shepheardes Calender* or traces of English interest in the Spanish Renaissance diverted attention from the intent and nature of the "Eglogs" themselves, and it was not until the appearance of an essay by Paul E. Parnell in 1961 that an accurate account of the work was published.[8]

To Parnell, Googe's pastorals represent the confrontation of "English morality and Latin sophistication," especially as the latter flourished in Renaissance Italy: "he wrote the *Eglogs* as a sort of refutation of the pastoral tradition" insofar as that tradition comprised an idyllic celebration of the beauties and complexities of love, and "his determination to purge the pastoral of its evil tendencies in fact required the destruction of the form."[9] In its place, Parnell shows, Googe substituted "a stern and resolute sermon," coherent and rhetorically complete.[10] But Parnell allows that Googe is "following the lead of Mantuan, who had . . . used the pastoral for the celebration of Christian ideals,"[11] and notes the many parallels between Mantuan's ideas and those of the "Eglogs," as Googe adapts his main model to his purpose.[12]

It has since been shown both that pastoralism was by no means alien to the northern countries and that the eclogue everywhere through the Middle Ages and into the Renaissance was much less the home of the amatory Arcadianism Googe repudiates than of the moral commentary and religious vision he stresses.[13] Although the "Eglogs" undeniably issue in the sermon against love that Parnell elucidates, they are quintessentially pastoral in the way they arrive at the understanding of love

on which the homily is based. In all its many forms the pastoral strives
to gain a perspective on the problems of real experience by regarding
them from a clarifying point of view, or, in Empson's phrase, by "putting the complex into the simple."[14] Thus the life of the city can be
observed and judged by implicit or explicit comparison with the life of
the country; thus the tangled issue of poetic love can be unraveled
through the agency of traditional literary shepherds, whose amours
provide a simplified model for study and whose homely wisdom,
rooted in time-honored ideals of shepherdship and the basic truths of
nature—the seasons of the landscape and the seasons of life—places
the question in the light of a larger truth.

By putting the pastoral to work in the effort to solve the problem of
literary love, Googe constructed a singularly unified set of eclogues.
Though he did not achieve the coherent design of *The Shepheardes
Calender*, Googe did demonstrate the utility of exploring a single issue
from the multiple viewpoints of a pastoral series.[15] The "Eglogs" are a
dialectical treatise on love, its dangers, its irrationality, and its sinfulness, employing the varied resources of the genre to analyze love, to
define it, to show it in action, and to identify one alternative to it.

The most obvious hallmark of pastoral poetry is its rural setting. In
Googe's eclogues, the shepherds' comments on the season, weather, and
time of day, along with other bits of pastoral stage-business, are rather
perfunctory, although charming, and serve mainly to identify the
genre of the poems. An astrological-vegetative *reverdie* that opens the
first eclogue is of this nature, but through its close association of precise
booklearning with homely observation it also establishes at the outset
the crucial pastoral juxtaposition of the rustic with the urbane. The
eclogues that follow study the sophisticated conventions of poetic love
from the perspective of simple country life.

A conditioned reflex in Western culture prompts poets to begin their
poems about love in a springtime setting. Googe binds the traditional
background into the main argument. Winter, young Daphnes says, has
held our discourse in check, but now that spring has come we both
may and should tell our shepherds' tales. Amintas, older and wiser,
should properly be the first to speak. Although he considers himself
beyond "spring time tales," Amintas nevertheless agrees, out of respect
for Daphnes' father, to set forth "the state of Loue" (I, 17, 21; p. 24).[16]
His hesitations enable Googe to define the occasion precisely: a tradition is being passed down from one generation to the next.

Intoning an invocation to Cupid to fill him with poet's fury, Amintas lays down the doctrine of poetic love point for point, thus stating the thesis of Googe's dialectic. The subsequent eclogues provide the antithesis by following out some of its implications. But the old shepherd is no apologist for Cupid. He describes love as a disease caught by looking at pretty faces. Its symptoms are the usual physical and psychological disorders of the lover. His imagery for love is uniformly repulsive, including not only the familiar ideas of fire, pain, entrapment, and servitude, but also a more forceful view of the lover as poisoned, his blood infected and seething with corruption, his senses in decay. Despite his judgment of love, Amintas can only warn his young friend to "Take heade of vewynge faces longe" and to spurn pederasty (I, 74, 76; p. 29). In gratitude, Daphnes presents him with a sweet-tuned whistle that once belonged to his father. The frank and reasonable fellowship between the shepherds contrasts with the sufferings of love which Amintas has just described and which will be brought to life in the next eclogue.

"Egloga secunda" is a mere thirty-six lines, but it provides an important step in the progress of Googe's attack on love. A young shepherd impaled on Cupid's dart, Dametas is so entangled in the paradoxes of love that he can see no way out save suicide, a way that he takes at the end of his monologue. Peirce makes a strong case that Googe wrote this eclogue bearing in mind the second part of "Harpelus complaynt . . ." in Tottel's *Miscellany* (No. 181). The sufferings of Harpelus are treated with a lightness of tone that renders them simply picturesque, and his death for love remains an ornate conjecture. In Googe's adaptation lightness gives way to burlesque, and Dametas, even in his onstage demise, becomes the object not of amused sympathy but of satirical opprobrium.[17]

Dametas has, he feels, performed his part of the love-game very well, but his lady ignores his service and requites his flames of love with the flame of "depe disdaynfull Ire"; clearly it grieves her to see him healthy: "Thou seest her mynd, why fearst thou than? / *Dametas* for to dye?" (II, 15–16, 20; p. 32). Thus, reasoning incontrovertibly from the premises of love doctrine such as that just set forth by Amintas, Dametas talks himself into suicide as the ultimate act of service to his beloved. Throughout the poem Googe repeats Dametas' proposition, adjusting the interval to become shorter and shorter as the tension mounts to the final cry, "O Shephardes all, be Wytnesses, / *Dametas* here doth dye." We have already learned, however, that "no man els is bye" (II, 27; p. 33). It could be a touching scene: a poor deluded

shepherd, forlorn, surrounded by his sheep, wailing out his swansong
at the edge of some stream or pond ("this flud"—II, 4; p. 31), into
which he then plunges himself to drown. But the pathos is pushed to
melodrama, and the ironic light of mockery cuts through the senti-
mental gloom. "Draw nere O mighty Herd of beasts," he calls to his
sheep:

> Resolue your Brutisshe eies to teares
>   and all togyther crye,
> Bewayle the wofull ende of Loue,
>   *Dametas* nowe must dye. (II, 27–30; p. 33)[18]

In the third eclogue Dametas is called a "Martir." The term
advances Googe's treatise by sharpening the definition of love and preparing the way for its final rejection in the eighth eclogue. Dametas
has died because of his faithfulness to the rites and rituals of what has
unavoidably become, with a dogma in the first eclogue and a martyr
in the second, a veritable religion of love. In both the third and fourth
eclogues shepherds suppose Dametas to be a saint in heaven, apothe-
osized for his loyalty and courage. That they are as mistaken as poor
Dametas, however, will presently appear.

The narrow focus on love of the first two eclogues dissolves in the
third, where Googe introduces a satire on the manners and morals of
the town and an allegory on ecclesiastical abuses—both de rigueur in
the Mantuan eclogue. Most aggregations of eclogues, even the highly
unified *Shepheardes Calender*, treat a variety of subjects. Googe finds
a way to imitate this characteristic of his genre without interrupting
the steady development of his theme,[19] for the broader concerns of the
third eclogue establish an ethical context that validates his attack on
love.

Asked for a report on the town where he has sojourned, Coridon
replies that vice has supplanted virtue at every level. The root of the
trouble is that true nobility no longer exists among the ruling class,
which is now composed of crafty upstart carters and churls: "Fisshe
bred vp, in durtye Pooles, / wyll euer stynke of mudde" (III, 42; p.
37). The presence of all these "dunghill knights" (III, 53; p. 38) is no
surprise, because "the chiefest man" in town is now *Coridon* no
kynne to me, / a Neteherd thother daye" (III, 55–56; p. 38). The
account of this usurping ruler's offenses anticipates Spenser's July
eclogue. Although good shepherds have previously led the sheep out of

the "Stynkyng dales" to feed "on pleasant Hylles," the new ruler has
led them back, "And to theyr old corrupted Grasse, / enforceth them
to cleaue" (III, 61, 64; p. 39). The obvious reference to the Marian
reaction continues in remarks on the burnings and exiles of "yᵉ Shephardes good" (III, 67; p. 39), culminating in the deaths of Daphnes and
Alexis, that is, Latimer and Ridley.[20]

Googe's brief essay in topical satire and ecclesiastical allegory is
more remarkable for avoiding the usual obscurity of such writing than
for the force of its strokes. By letting them fall nearly a decade too late,
Googe managed to avoid setting himself up against his patron Cecil
and the reinstated Protestant establishment to which he adhered. But
the passage assumes its full meaning only as part of the entire third
eclogue.

Before discussing the town's estate, the shepherds have recalled the
"Martir" Dametas and remarked upon an old ram belonging to Coridon. Like Dametas, the ram has run into trouble with love. Taking a
liking to the "Yewes / of pleasaunte forme" in the herd Dametas
bequeathed to Titirus, he got into a fight with their proper ram and is
now lamed and "waylynge" (III, 13, 22; p.35). His pursuit of animal
pleasure is described in the terminology of courtly love: "pleasaũt
dames," "woer," "suche happes in loue there be" (III, 15, 21; p. 35).
The combination parodies the love-religion that has just claimed
Dametas' life, associating it with the lust that is merely natural in the
unfortunate ram but, when unchecked by reason, deeply reprehensible
in man.

After describing the town, whose degeneracy likewise stems from
religious error, the poem concludes with a celebration of rustic life. But
there is no trace of idyllic indulgence: Googe's pastoral retreat is severe
and moralistic. Coridon turns his back on the pride, cruelty, and vice
of the town, confident that the sinners will feel God's scourge in time.
The hard comforts of the country are best. As a rainstorm gathers, he
invites Menalcas and his flock to take shelter in his cottage:

> Som Chestnuts haue I there in store
>   with Cheese and pleasaunt whaye,
> God sends me Vittayles for my nede,
>   and I synge Care awaye. (III, 82–86; pp. 40–41)

"Egloga tertia" thus establishes an association between the sinful condition of the town and the sinful passion of poetic love. The truly good

and human life can be found neither in the courts of ambition nor in the courts of love. Both the corruption of the town and the sufferings of love are the products of heresy.

In the fourth eclogue the cult of love comes into direct confrontation with religious truth when the shade of Dametas returns not from the company of saints but from the torments of hell.[21] When he appears, sheep flee in terror; when he speaks, "a stynkyng smoke" (IV, 19; p. 43) comes out of his mouth; and, when he is finished speaking, he is carried off by "an vglye Fende, / With lothsome Clawes" (IV, 49–50; p. 45). This comic sensationalism prevents any sympathy for Dametas from obscuring the lesson he has to teach. In pursuing the love of his lady, he explains, he has committed the unpardonable sin of suicide and therefore now suffers the torture of flames much worse than the flames of love with which he formerly burned.

The progression from love to suicide to hell-flame elaborates the danger of the amatory heresy. By allowing passion to usurp the place of his reason, Dametas has rendered himself an animal like Coridon's ram, a destruction of the self anterior to and reflected in his suicide. In terms of the opposition between true religion and the religion of love, Dametas has, as he says (IV, 45–46; p. 45), placed his lady in the position that should be God's. Contrary to the doctrine of poetic love, he now sees that, had he saved a place for God in his heart—like the speaker of "To Maystresse A."—he would have been able to master his affections.

The next three eclogues support and expand the case against love. All manifest Spanish influence: the fifth and seventh directly follow Montemayor,[22] while the sixth tacks the material borrowed in the fifth onto the frame of the "Eglogs." In the *Diana* the familiar story Googe took for his fifth eclogue is a courtly intrigue. Felismena, disguised as "Valerius," loves Don Felix (Googe's Faustus) but must pay court for him to Celia (Googe's Claudia). Celia falls in love with "Valerius" and dies in a trance when she discovers that her love is not requited; Felix, in despair, drops out of sight; and the lonely Felismena is left to wander about the countryside as a shepherdess, telling her tale. Later she will be reunited with her beloved. In Googe's adaptation, Claudia commits suicide after being spurned by Valerius, who is really a boy, so that when Faustus absconds he leaves no forlorn lady behind him. It is Faustus himself who turns up tending a flock in "Egloga sexta," apparently aware only of Claudia's rejection of his suit, not of her death.

Undeterred by the striking differences in form and tone between

Montemayor's Arcadian romance in prose and his own pastoral sequence, Googe tried to borrow only what fit his needs. His pared-down version dispenses with the fine shades of emotion and irony explored by Montemayor and emphasizes instead the progression of narrative events and their causal relationship. In case the borrowed material might seem out of place among his "Eglogs," Googe announces at the outset that this is a *court* story, set in the corrupt world castigated in the third eclogue, and also "a desperate Acte of Loue" (V, 5; p. 47) like the suicide of Dametas. Its disastrous outcome is the predictable result of love and duplicity, and its moralized import sustains the general theme of the "Eglogs."[23]

The sixth eclogue contains a widely noted translation of some lines from Sannazaro's *Arcadia* that came to Googe through a Spanish intermediary, the second eclogue of Garcilaso de la Vega. But, as Peirce has shown, Googe mainly relies on a selection of passages from Ovid's *Remedia Amoris*.[24] In the fourth eclogue the shade of Dametas names reason as the key to escaping the snares of love and turning to the true religion, but he does not explain how it should be employed. Now Felix performs this service by lecturing the jilted Faustus on the remedies of love. After the first motion of reason, which perceives the folly and pain of love, the prescription consists of removing from the senses the object of the love-fixation and anything that might recall her, and then, to prevent the fancy from drifting back, of avoiding idleness and of keeping occupied with other things until, at length, forgetfulness frees the mind from the "Yoke of Louers Lawe" (VI, 86; p. 59). Googe can use only a small part of his source, since Ovid's attitudes are alien to his moral frame of reference. A long passage on the distractions of the countryside (11. 169ff.), however, is particularly appropriate. It briefly mentions bird-snaring; Googe uses the lines from Garcilaso to flesh it out, then returns to Ovid to suggest fishing as a further distraction. But Googe develops the idea of a country sojourn into a pastoral antagonism to the town that the citified Ovid does not share, and when Felix refers to the "strōger Medycines" (VI, 88; p. 59) he will reveal to Faustus in their next conversation, he alludes not to the cynical strategies of self-deception Ovid suggests in those pages of his poem that Googe discreetly passes over but to the homily Cornix will pronounce in "Egloga octaua."

The doctrine of Amintas in the first eclogue was painful and despairing; its equally traditional counterpart in the discourse of Felix points toward freedom and hope. All the remedies he mentions depend on

the lover's retreat from the court to the countryside, where simple pastoral beauties and pleasures can supplant the destructive attractions of
the lady. For similar but broader reasons, shepherds in the third and
eighth eclogues give thanks for the simplicity of their rustic estate.

The seventh eclogue obscures the distinction between the court,
love, sin, and heresy on the one side and the country, virtue, reason,
and the true religion on the other, but it makes a small thematic contribution nonetheless. The first scenes of the *Diana* consist primarily of
charge and countercharge about men's and women's constancy
between two shepherds and a shepherdess, all of whom have been dis-
appointed in love. The discussion, in the original a prelude to the shepherdess's tale, ends inconclusively in Googe's paraphrase. Evidently
these unfortunate lovers will get nowhere until they stop blaming the
opposite sex for their troubles and conquer passion in their own hearts.
But the tone is wrong: the speakers do not writhe in the flames of love
but give instead through their urbane chatter the impression of being
fairly happy in their lot. At the start one shepherd does praise his companion for rising above his own griefs enough to comfort others. His
charitable attitude links the eclogue into the series by pointing the way
out of the hopeless imbroglios that result from placing trust in fickle
lovers and toward the final resolution of trust in the constant God.

The eighth eclogue fuses the stress on reason and the pastoral retreat
developed through the sequence into a general Christian stoicism,[25]
which, charged with the rhetoric of the allegorical homily, issues in a
remarkable sermon against the heresy of love. Many images introduced in the previous eclogues reappear, so that the final poem provides not only a thematic resolution but also an artistic conclusion to
the "Eglogs" as a whole. The setting and occasion recall the dialogue
of Daphnes and Amintas in the first eclogue. Cornix and Coridon shade
themselves from the sweltering dog-day weather under a "pleasaunte
Brodeleaued Beech" near a "springing foūtain cleare" (VIII, 7; p. 70),
which, they say, God has placed there to defend them from the heat.
Light of heart and purse, they have no fear of "the tomblyng world"
(VIII, 10; p. 70), and feel impelled to sing "Not of the wretched Louers
lyues, / but of the immortall kynge," who has granted them the good
fortune "to lyue / in symple Shephards state" (VIII, 12, 16; p. 71).
Googe carefully connects love with paganism, and bases its repudiation
mainly on this association. "O Shephards leaue *Cupidoes* Camp," Cornix urges, "the end wherof is vyle" (VIII, 21; p. 71). None of the pagan
gods, whom he mocks at length,

> Can the defende: as God wyll do,
>> for they were synfull fooles,
> Whō fyrst yᵉ blynd hye wytted Greke
>> brought in to wyse mens Scooles. (VIII, 55–56; p. 74)

To recount the fate of the man who follows lust and does not return to the true God, Googe develops an allegory that parodies the Petrarchist image of the lover wandering in a ship through stormy seas. God turns his face away from the persistent sinner, who sets sail on "the seas of sin" in "vyces Barge" (VIII, 79, 76; p. 76), running before the wind of affection with Pleasure at the helm.[26] Planning to repent only in his old age, he decks himself with costly clothes at court and tries his hand at war. Mars leads of course to Venus. He sports himself and lords it over his underlings, enjoying himself to the hilt. But his luck soon changes, "For death (that old deuouryng Wolf) . . . Coms saylyng fast, in Galley blacke . . ." (VIII, 99–100; p. 78). A battle ensues worthy of a good morality play, ending with one of Googe's more felicitous turns:

> Thē farewell all. The wretched man
>> with Caryen Corse doth lye,
> Whō Deth hymself flyngs ouer bord,
>> amyd the Seas of syn,
> The place wher late, he swetly swam
>> now lyes he drowned in. (VIII, 108–10; p. 79)

The "Syndrownd soule," like the shade of the self-drowned Dametas, is carried off to hell by "a Monster . . . begot of Due Desert" (VIII, 111–13; p. 79), and the shepherds, after stressing that this is the end facing all those who follow lust and live in sin rather than loving and fearing God, hurry home to avoid an approaching storm.

Googe's treatise is now complete: like the corruptions of the town, love has been proved a religious error. The alternative to love and its perils is the same as the alternative to those other sins—the simple life of reason, humility, faith, and self-denial. The pastoral dichotomy between country and city—and all they stand for—has provided a moral polarity within which love is readily classified and shown to be quite unattractive by contrast with the beautiful pastoral simplicity against which it is set.

The idea of using pastoral poetry against poetic love was not original with Googe. Palingenius had done it in a passage of bold burlesque (see above, pp. 38–39), and Mantuan had contrasted "honest love" with "insane love" in two narratives, the former ending in marriage, the latter in grief. Mantuan's moral *sententiae* and exhortations resemble the preachments of Googe, but his presentation of the doctrine has less impact. Mantuan's Amyntas runs lamenting through the wilderness until he dies of exposure and starvation—a victim of love, but not exactly a suicide. Although he is lectured about the sinfulness of his passion, this idea is not embodied in his fate, for after his death he is praised by the very shepherds who have lectured him, and the reader is left with the impression that he is in heaven.[27] Googe invites his reader to bite the baited hook of Dametas' martyrdom, and then, in the fourth eclogue, he pulls it home with the shepherd's return from hell. Googe's eclogues surpass Mantuan's in structure even as they follow them in theme. Mantuan's attack on the decadent Roman Curia, for example, is the likely inspiration for Googe's description of the town's estate. But while Mantuan presents his satire for what it is worth and moves on to other matters, Googe binds the corruptions of the town and court into a paradigm of false and true religions, virtues and vices, order and disorder, reason and inordinate affection.

Googe's analysis of love is thorough and his attack on it severe. That he does not somehow reconstruct it is a limitation of the "Eglogs" and of all his poetry, for love cannot be adequately replaced by religion or an ascetic virtue. But Googe's single-mindedness yields an unequivocal statement of the impasse between poetic love and moral philosophy that exercised sixteenth-century poets. In "Cupido Conquered," the dream vision next to be discussed, he worked out an allegory of the mind's liberation from the snares of the same immoral love defined in the "Eglogs." In the process he set forth in symbolic terms a critical rationale for the antiamatory poetry so characteristic of Reformation England.

II   *"Cupido Conquered"*

When C. S. Lewis considers "Cupido Conquered" in *The Allegory of Love*, he is struck by "its complete fidelity to the oldest models in this kind."[28] Lewis calls the *Roman de la Rose* a "germinal" book, "a parent, begetting offspring at once like and unlike itself."[29] "Cupido Conquered" is a scion of this ancient line, but although many generations removed from its noble ancestor, in several ways it stands unmarked by the three-century evolution of the form.

Why did Googe in 1563 produce such an apparent anachronism? At least in part because he was again trying to write in a genre whose standard features he knew well and at the same time to use it for special purposes of his own. His long "Dreame," although by his own admission shoddily finished,[30] is no less resourceful a response to the problem of poetic love than the "Eglogs." He does not seem to have confined himself to imitating any single work, old or new, but rather, after examining many poems, to have settled on the essential features of his genre, and he undoubtedly expected his readers to recognize his perfect fidelity to the most venerable traditions of the kind.

The medieval dream-poem convention lived on well into the sixteenth century. Dunbar, Douglas, Lindsay, Skelton, and Hawes employed it, as did the author of the Prologue to *The Court of Venus*. Sackville's "Induction" to the *Mirror for Magistrates* is contemporaneous with Googe's poem, and they are not the last of the line. Perhaps interest in the form was sustained by the popular volumes of Chaucer issued during the century, which contained not only *The Romaunt of the Rose* and Chaucer's own visionary poems but also many apocryphal love allegories and dreams.[31] Googe may also have seen several dream poems in Spanish by the Marqués of Santillana, whose proverbs he was to translate in 1579,[32] but he had to go no further than Palingenius to find a model for dramatizing ideas and learning as visionary action and discourse. Googe's use of the genre was fully in harmony with the practice of medieval writers from the fourteenth century on, whom it served as "a device for expressing the poet's consciousness of himself as poet," especially in regard to the matter of love.[33] In his eclogues Googe explored love in objective terms; in his dream vision he deals with a purportedly personal instance of a poet wrestling with Cupid's snares. The immediate impulse for rejecting love comes not from an awareness of love's irrationality, although that awareness is presupposed, but from a practical conflict of desires: the sufferings of love have kept the poet from writing and his Muses are calling.

Briefly, "Cupido Conquered" proceeds as follows: wandering forth on a spring day, the poet finds a fountain under a laurel tree. He falls asleep and dreams that he is accosted by Mercury, who, after some conversation, leads him to a castle where Diana holds her court. Cupid invades Diana's realm, and the poet sees an army led by Hippolytus capture Cupid and put his forces to flight. The dreamer then awakes and writes the poem about his dream.

Like the "Eglogs," the poem begins with the obligatory *reverdie*. The colors of the trees and a profusion of hawthorn blossoms are sig-

nificant: white indicates purity or virginity; green was the color of
amorous passion for the courtly love tradition.[34] The poet, seeking in
the diversions of the outdoors some relief from the pain of separation
from his beloved, takes delight in the singing of birds that excel
Amphion and "Sir *Orpheus*" as musicians. A picture of Orpheus's
probable reaction to these singers further associates them with poetry
and, like the similar account of Plautus and Terence's chagrin in "Of
Edwardes of the Chappell" (see above, p. 56), establishes an ironic
tone: "I rather iudge the thracian wold . . ." (1. 25; p. 142)[35] have
thrown away his harp in anger. The tongue-in-cheek remark enables
Googe, as always, to use the mythological reference without appearing
absurd. Thoroughly traditional in substance, the first thirty-four lines
of "Cupido Conquered" are modeled specifically on the first part of
Surrey's "Complaint of a louer, that defied loue, and was by loue after
the more tormented" (Tottel, No. 5). Surrey's speaker also walks out in
the spring to ease his heart and to hear the birds. Although their song
cheers him, he realizes enviously that the birds are rejoicing because
nature has given them leave to choose their mates and love freely. He
curses love and tries to throw off Cupid's yoke but soon regrets his
attempt when he finds that it cannot be done and that it will be worse
for him now because Cupid will not even help him with his courtship:

> A miror let me be vnto ye louers all:
> Striue not with loue: for if ye do, it will ye thus befall.

Googe takes up the challenge and sets out to prove that Cupid *can* be
overthrown. His imitation of Surrey's poem, besides providing a fitting
prologue for the dream vision, serves to recall a statement of the contrary view.

Next he draws together several further motives familiar in love
visions. The poet watches the singing birds until he notices "a stately
Lawrell tree" (1. 35; p. 143) placed so beautifully beside a spring that
"Dame Nature" seems to have been showing off in planting it (1. 37;
p. 143). The tree and the fountain bristle with literary associations, of
which the speaker is aware:

> For sure I thynke, it was the place,
>   wherein *Narcissus* dyed,
> Or els the Well, to which was turnd
>   poore *Biblis* whyle she cryed. (11. 57–58; p. 145)

Googe does not miss a chance to pursue his vendetta. Narcissus and Byblis are not merely unfortunate lovers who suffered from their love: their names suggest subtly repugnant perversions—Narcissus loved himself; Byblis loved her twin brother.

When the dreamer in the *Roman de la Rose* peers down into the fountain of Narcissus, he sees reflected in two crystals the whole garden and especially the Rosebud he will seek. The crystals represent the lady's eyes, and it is at this moment that the dreamer falls in love, immediately suffering the wounds of Cupid's arrows.[36] In "Cupido Conquered" the poet is already in love, but what he sees has definite symbolic overtones. Within the fountain are reflected green trees, white blossoms, and a choir of birds—a natural garden now solidly connected with the allegorical garden of the *Roman,* where birdsong also provides a hypnotically charming background. What strikes the eye of Googe's poet is not a beloved rose but the tokens of passion, chastity, and song, combined in setting suggestive of traditional visionary poetry.

The glare of the sun forces him to take shelter beneath the laurel tree. Lulled by weariness, strange fumes from the spring, the music of the birds, and the influence of "woddy Nimphes," he soon falls into a "slumbre deepe" (11. 63, 65; p. 145), and the second part of the poem begins. Mercury, dressed in white, accosts the dreamer, and the exchange discussed above (p. 16) ensues. The poet's trouble is partly reticence, but not entirely. "Bycause they know the blynded God / hath somethyng pearced the," Mercury says, the Muses have commanded him to show the poet something that "shall gyue the occasion good, / with ioyfull mynde to wryght" (11. 104, 106; pp. 148–49). Idleness not only brings on but also results from the enervation of love. The praiseworthy work that the Muses inspire him to is the key to the poet's escape from the vicious circle. The encounter with Mercury thus binds together Googe's moral and artistic themes.

The god tells the astonished dreamer to follow him; wings sprout on his sides; and off they fly to "a Gorgyous Castell" (1. 117; p. 150). Cautioning him to "note what thou doost se" (1. 120; p. 150), Mercury hurries away, leaving the dreamer frightened and alone, cursing his guide for having deserted him. Still, he decides, "hap what hap wyll to me" (1. 134; p. 151), to approach the castle.

In a line Googe nods his acknowledgment to the conventional description of the exterior and makes nothing of the usually symbolic entrance into the palace itself. But after his dreamer nervously strolls

in, Googe does full justice to one of the most fascinating and variously
exploited features of the genre, the paintings on the walls.[37] Many
authors took advantage of such frescoes to retell mythical or legendary
tales. In "Cupido Conquered" the paintings indicate to the dreaming
poet who it is that dwells in the palace and remind him of something
he needs to know. He finds himself in what amounts to Diana's trophy
room. There is a picture of Acteon; one showing Orion in his discomfiture, subscribed, "Accounte thy selfe but lost, yf that / thou bearste
a lecherous Hart" (1. 153; p. 152); and "many Storyes more" about
"What fearefull haps to many men, / for lust vncleane befell" (11.
161–62; p. 153).

Suddenly, a messenger, "blowyng fast for want of breath" (1. 168;
p. 154), rushes past the dreamer, who follows him into Diana's presence chamber. In a shining robe of silver-white, the goddess sits on a
high throne surrounded by her court. Among the throng are chaste but
not virgin women such as Dido and Lucretia; famous virgins, led by
Hippolytus; and a trio of personified abstractions—Continence,
Labour, and Abstinence.

The fraternization of mythological and legendary figures with personified abstractions is not unusual in medieval and Renaissance allegory, where virtues or vices are often symbolized by their practitioners.
Thus Diana, the chaste goddess, comes to represent the principle or
ideal of Chastity, just as Venus, who is mentioned but never appears,
looms over the poem as the erotic principle. So Hippolytus stands
against Cupid; the latter represents the action of lust in the soul, the
former the counter-action of the ideal of chastity.[38] Continence,
Labour, and Abstinence are concomitant virtues to chastity, and
although Continence is not described (the proposition does present
some difficulty), Googe pictures Labour as a laborer, Abstinence as one
who has abstained. Later he envisions one of Cupid's lieutenants,
"Exces," in an effectively repulsive passage anticipating Spenser's
description of Gluttony, as "A Lubbour great . . . full trust with guts"
(11. 301, 305; p. 165).

The messenger falls on his knees before Diana and bursts into a plea
for aid against a terrible invader, whose army is ravaging her realm.
As captain, Cupid rides with his golden bow and a quiver of poisonous
arrows in a chariot. He has sacked a number of Diana's forts and slain
many with his mysterious darts. The wounds he inflicts fester and
spread venom to the heart. The victims burn with fever or seek relief

in suicide—drowning themselves, leaping from houses, or hanging themselves "full thycke" on rafters or trees (11. 219–22; p. 158). "Nothyng abashde" (1. 232; p. 159), Hippolytus knows his duty and, reassuring the frightened ladies of the court, vows to bring the rampaging enemy back in chains.

Diana charges Hippolytus to raise an army and meet the invaders in a full epic battle. Here "Cupido Conquered" reaches back to the archetype of another literary tradition, the *Psychomachia* of Prudentius. One of the goriest conflicts in Prudentius's poem is the slaying of Libido by Pudicitia,[39] a victory which is possible because all human flesh shares in the nature of the virgin birth and may be purified by Baptism. Prudentius's theological rationale differs from the moral-psychological scheme of "Cupido Conquered" as much as the bloody details that adorn the *Psychomachia* differ from Googe's generalized reports of who strikes blows and who then falls.

After a tearful farewell, Hippolytus sallies forth. Soldiers, "All armed braue in Corsletes white" (1. 278; p. 163), rally to his trumpet and prepare to meet the enemy, whose general approaches, scattering flames in all directions and leading behind him a thousand bleeding hearts. The dreamer hears Hippolytus harangue his soldiers, praising their virtue and manhood while disparaging the disorderly array of their adversaries, and the inevitable pattern of battle unfolds. The soldiers of Labour overcome those of Idlenes, and the two captains fight it out until Idlenes falls. Labour then goes to the aid of "Syr *Abstinence*" and together "the gresye Hoaste, / of Glottonye they slewe" (11. 341–42; p. 168), as Cupid's troops take to their heels.

Googe renders the precise moment of the victory of the powers of chastity within the soul through a familiar image descended from the *Phaedrus*. When Hippolytus strikes Cupid's charioteer down from his post and "A Souldier stoute of *Reasons* bande" (1. 356; p. 169) takes his place, the rational will is reining in the appetites and holding lust in check. The soul, formerly in disarray because of the unrestrained triumph of the erotic impulse, returns to its proper order.

Cupid reminds his conquerors that he could very well have won the battle, and Googe realistically leaves his fate undetermined. The poem ends with a passage of pleasant recapitulation that artfully rounds off the narration. The dreamer awakes in confusion but soon recognizes the fountain and the laurel. After watching the sunset and the birds preparing for rest, he returns home to a restless bed. But:

> When *Phebus* rose to passe the tyme,
>   and passe my gryefe awaye
> I toke my Pen and pend the Dreame
>   that made my Muses staye. (11. 387–88; p. 172)

Despite the outcome of the psychomachy, the poet still suffers amatory symptoms—grief and sleeplessness. To resolve in the mind to cast off love by exercising the rational will (to defeat love in the arena of the soul) does not result in immediate freedom from pain: love and lust act on the body as well as the soul. As for Faustus in "Egloga sexta," the cure will be gradual at best. But by rising in the morning and setting to work, the poet takes a positive step. He writes "to passe the tyme," that is, to avoid idleness, which is, as Felix explains, the first step toward overcoming love's torments.

We have seen that the *locus classicus* for this conception of the role of idleness in matters of love is in Ovid. Googe acknowledges his indebtedness in a marginal note to the brief gnome "To Alexander Neuell" (p. 117), a translation of verses 139–40 and 162–63 of the *Remedia Amoris*. Neville's reply succinctly states the psychological mechanism that operates in "Cupido Conquered" and indicates its moral implications, even using two of the same epithets—"Drowsy Idlenes" and "vyle exces." Perhaps, then, we should pronounce "Cupido Conquered" and its allegory needless elaboration, a bothersome interposition between the reader and the kernel of meaning it buries.[40] But Googe's dream does not simply expand an aphorism. Like the overheard thought of his best short poems, it shadows forth the interplay of desire and knowledge that, according to the traditional psychology, leads to human choice.

"Cupido Conquered" may be called, as Lewis calls the *Roman de la Rose*, a *radical allegory*, that is, a poem whose allegorical surface can be rendered "without confusion, but not without loss," into a consistent literal story.[41] Externalization of inner conflicts is the essence of the mode, which presupposes the existence of a character or characters within whom the conflicts are really taking place, such as the lover and his mistress in the *Roman*.

Googe's poem can be readily translated into literal narration. A poet has fallen in love and lost his mistress. The loss, added to his reluctance for fear of adverse criticism, has rendered him unable to write. He sets forth one spring day to distract himself from his woe. The conventional landscape cannot be translated, but this is not necessary, for the externalization of the poet's inner conflict begins only when he falls asleep. As the messenger of the gods, Mercury often stands for eloquence, but let us say that here he represents the poet's *desire* to be eloquent, his poetic ambition. This ambition spurs him on by reminding him of others' successes and instilling a hope for eventual fame, and drives him to the point—the gate of Diana's castle—where he can see a way to overcome his major obstacle, love, and so get on with his work. When Hippolytus triumphs over Cupid, the more chaste and more ambitious impulses of the poet's soul get the upper hand on his debilitating erotic desires; on the morrow he can write again.

Certain other elements of the poem fit the pattern. For instance, the pomp of the mustered court of Diana set beside the ragged army of Cupid and its devastation of the countryside can represent the poet's knowledge of the dignity and nobility of chastity balanced with his perception of the repulsiveness and destructive effect of love. The bookish and derivative frescoes play a similar role: the poet has learned what he knows from ancient authors. Far from just decking a moral precept with gratuitous ornamentation, then, "Cupido Conquered" presents the externalized story of how and why a poet, meditating his case on a spring afternoon, makes up his mind to cast off the tyranny of love over his spirit and return to his work.

The fountain, laurel tree, birds, and May weather purport to be objects of the actual world and exert their symbolic force only outside the radical allegory. Googe includes them as obligatory stage properties of his genre and exploits the literary associations they recall to the poet by suggesting that the dream appears to him under their mysterious influence. It is only natural that a scholarly poet, having found in the real world a place so similar to the settings of the old visionary poems he knew, should one way or another conceive an analogous dream vision for himself.

The dream finally teaches not only how to overcome love in the soul but how to deal with it in poetry. "Cupido Conquered" acts out in detail the response Googe made to the problem presented by his artistic conservatism and his desire to use poetry for moral suasion; it is a poem about poetry, a piece of literary theory. The vision sent him by the Muses shows that, by portraying love defeated, one can treat the traditional subject in the traditional genres without abdicating moral responsibility. As we have seen, this is exactly Googe's strategy in his short love poems and in the "Eglogs."

Although Googe wrote "Cupido Conquered" in precise imitation of the traditional dream-vision allegory, court of love, and psychomachy, he thoroughly transformed the conventions to advance his theory. William Dunbar, for example, presents the opposition between love and reason in *The Goldyn Targe*, but unlike Googe he does not take sides. While he shows Reason powerless in the presence of Beauty, his forces of love seem charming rather than dangerous; his evident purpose is to display eloquence in celebration of traditional poetic love. The moral concern of "Cupido Conquered" is entirely foreign to Dunbar's short poem and to Stephen Hawes's encyclopedic *Pastime of Pleasure* as well. It does find oblique expression, however, in *The Palice of Honour* by Gavin Douglas, where the dreamer encounters Diana poorly attended and then a glorious triumph of Venus. Insulted by his song on the sufferings of love, the goddess forces him to debase his art by composing a more acceptable lyric, and it is only seven hundred lines later when she enlists him to translate the story of her son Aeneas that Douglas finds an appropriate way to serve her.[42] These late medieval allegories deal in general types to describe what is real in the abstract, idealistic sense. Love incontrovertibly exists and so finds representation in the usual ways. Googe is less concerned with what is real than with what is good, or rather what one should do. Thus he builds his allegory around a single choice made by a particular man in a particular situation. Despite its conservatism of form, "Cupido Conquered" differs from these predecessors in much the same way that the "hybrid" Tudor interludes and "virtue plays" differ from "full-scope" medieval morality plays.[43] Googe uses allegory to bring to life the elements that enter into the choice, disclosing their true nature as perceived by the moral sense. Cupid's army is by no means attractive, even though love is undeniably attractive in real life.

"Cupido Conquered" was not the only antiamorist dream vision of the early Elizabethan period, but despite its flaws it was the most artistically successful and morally coherent. The three dreams that begin *A poore Knight his Pallace of Priuate pleasures*,[44] for example, treat literary love as repulsive but irresistible and recommend marriage as a rather unappealing alternative. W. A.'s "A vision of rawe deuise, written to Fancies fellowes" tries to advance the general thesis of *A Speciall Remedie against the Furious force of lawless Loue*[45] that only God's grace can free the soul from lust; thus Reason's earnest preachments are wasted on the dreamer, who, unable to pray to the true God in a poem populated by imaginary deities, wanders off behind the black flag of Fancy. Googe, more optimistic in stressing the power of reason and self-control to purge the mind of love, gives a coherent narrative of some psychological depth and complexity, rather than an aborted sermon.

III   *"The Ship of Safegarde"*

The impulse to sermonize, however, exerted as great a temptation on Googe as did the siren song of fancy over the graceless dreamer in *A Speciall Remedie*, and his last and longest[46] original poem, although its allegorical imagery is developed beyond anything in "Cupido Conquered," attains no depth and no complexity. The title poem of *The Shippe of Safegarde* (1569)[47] takes as its theme the entire moral journey of the human soul toward salvation, a subject which challenges comparison to that of the first two books of *The Faerie Queene* and which overtaxes Googe's power to forge a unified poetic structure capable of embracing it. Although there are a number of noteworthy similarities in their symbolism, "The Ship of Safegarde" fails in important ways even to begin treating its material in the manner of *The Faerie Queene*, and suffers by comparison as an essay in allegory even with Googe's own previous effort.

Another reason why "The Ship of Safegarde" disappoints the expectations of a reader coming to it out of "Cupido Conquered" is suggested in Googe's dedication of the volume to his sisters-in-law "in these your yong and tender yeares" (sig. A2). Having lost the manuscript of a satire on present-day hypocrisy and a celebration of the saints of the primitive church intended for them, he hurriedly replaced it with this treatise on "the daūgers of this worlde" through which "the soule enclosed in the barke of sinfull fleshe wyth great hasard passeth" (sig. A2v). The resulting volume reflects not only Googe's didactic intent—both in the poem itself and in some prefatory verses to the reader on preferring the thorny strait path to salvation over the "smooth and plaine" highway to pleasure—but also an interest in the early church and some satiric impulses lingering from his previous endeavor. As we shall see in the next chapter, his adaptations of two miraculous legends from church history—included in *The Shippe of Safegarde* since Googe knows the young girls "delight in stories" (sig. A2v)—effectively convert ecclesiastical history into exemplary fiction. But serving the needs of his juvenile audience prevented Googe from fusing practical admonition, satire, and moral didacticism into a viable allegorical narrative in "The Ship of Safegarde" itself. In "Cupido Conquered" he explored a system of traditional myths and symbols until he discovered within it a resolution to a pressing problem about the moral potential of his art. In "The Ship of Safegarde" he speaks as one in possession of the answer rather than in search of it, embodying given wisdom in a simple analogy chosen no doubt for its ready accessibility to an audience of intellectual inferiors, who required, like the readers of Turbervile's *Plaine Path to Perfect Vertue*,[48] an elementary guide to life.

The poem nonetheless merits consideration, not only because it demonstrates the effects of such intentions on poetic composition (effects that would mark most "improving" literature written for children over the next two hundred years), but also because in it Googe once again took some hesitant steps down the paths followed by the great writers of subsequent decades, particularly Spenser, combining classical myth and Christian homily in an encyclopedic moral-allegorical poem.

The figure of man's life as the passage of a ship through stormy seas was common in antiquity and had been expounded from the pulpit for centuries as a vivid image of the plight of the faithful in a hostile world or of the soul buffeted by the surging tides of fleshly desire.[49] The ship itself was sometimes developed as the human body, the soul with its various faculties, the Church, or the state. Googe occasionally, as in the title and the dedication, refers to the *poem* as a ship, ill-rigged but able to carry the reader safely through. Usually, however, his ship remains an undifferentiated vehicle, capable of being guided with wisdom or folly, that brings the will from temptation to temptation. The nature of these perils and the ways to escape them comprise the main substance of his discourse, as Googe provides his reader with a map for the voyage of life.

Thirteen introductory stanzas stress the need for such a "Compasse" and "Carde" (2; sig. B1)[50] by expounding the basic figure. Any sailor on "the raging seas" must always busy himself about his navigation, minding his course and taking pleasure in nothing but fair winds. If he lets down his guard, his ship will hit the rocks and cast away "both frayght and foole and all" (3; sig. B1). And thus it is with "the will and fansie vayne of man" (4; sig. B1), Googe explains, that sails "the seas of fonde affection blinde, / . . . With sayles full thwackt with winde and lustie showe": only ten out of ten thousand find "The Hauen faire . . . of perfite ioye" (6–7; sig. B1v). To sail these dangerous seas we need "the helpe of holy sprite" (9; sig. B2). Invoking the same, therefore, as his Muse, Googe sets out to show "which way to runne, / What course to keepe, what daungers for to shunne" (13; sig. B2v).

The route leads past a series of islands and shoals that threaten to wreck "the soules that trauaile by" (13; sig. B2v). The massive golden rock of Pride looms up at the outset, studded with jewels and surrounded by "swelling sands" on which many ships, "forward puft with fonde vainglorious winde," have run aground (16–17; sig. B2v–B3). The mariner who finds "the chanell of lowlynesse," however, can steer clear of pride and may next approach Avarice, a "lothsome place" that attracts only those who delight in earthly dross (33, 35; sig. B5). The wise sailor will jettison his "bags and baggage" and "trauaile light" upon his way (50; sig. B7). "Enuious windes" now may blow the ship toward the rock of Detraction, "Encompast round with quicke and quiuering sand" (54, 53; sig. B7v). Inhabited by hissing serpents and giving off "poysned vapors," this "auncient enmy to the Barke of fame" is the ruin of those otherwise good sailors who indulge in gossip and slander (55, 56; sig. B7v). On the "foule great flat" (80; sig. C2v) of Gluttony, both bodily and spiritual health are destroyed. More readily entrancing is the next danger, "A gorgeous Ile, an earthly paradyse" (99; sig. C5), the seat of Fleshly Pleasure. Googe lavishes his most elaborate allegory on this central temptation, and we shall return to it later for a closer look. For the fortunate mariner who can "stay not gasing" and "sayle another way" (139; sig. D2), quite a different set of obstacles lies in wait—a triad of religious abuses. Heresy's smoothly polished surface lures even the best sailors onto its submerged rocks and has sometimes nearly brought "The Nauie faire of Christianitie" (144; sig. D2v) to entire destruction. The ornate island of Idolatry, studded with pyramids and lit by many torches, destroys not only "the Turkes and Paganes all" (170; sig. D6), but many Christians as well. "Let Paule thy Pilot be vpon these seas" (176; sig. D6v), Googe advises.[51] But it is "learned Chaucer that gem of Poetrie" who steers Googe himself past Hypocrisy, an island crowned by a statue of "Pope holye" borrowed from "the Romance of his Roses gaye" (183; sig. D7v) and described in thirty-six quoted lines. With these behind him, the mariner can take heart. No godly mind is likely to be troubled by the obvious "mischiefs" that ensue: Blasphemie, Cruelty, Hatred, Murder, Furie, Theft, Robbery, and a group of intellectual perversions including Sorcery, Astrology, and "infidelity" or the theory that the world runs at random. Like the Redcrosse Knight, who, having been retrieved from Orgoglio's castle, nearly dies in the Cave of Despaire, Googe's mariner must finally sail between the tower of Presumption and the black pit of Desperation before he sees the first of a series of "gracious markes" (207; sig. E3) that will lead him home. Following along from Prayer to Peace, Love, Mercy, and Patience, he finds Faith at last, "the chanell safe that leades to heauenly blisse" (214; sig. E4). The port itself, of course, cannot "be blasde by any mortall hand" (217; sig. E4v); therefore, Googe concludes, the reader will have to sail there to see it for himself.

"The Ship of Safegarde" thus navigates an orthodox and coherent voyage to salvation. The poem follows a rough division into mental, physical, and religious sins, with an appendix of minor evils and simple graces. Some sections remain perfunctory, but Googe elaborates each of the major temptations in generally parallel fashion. After describing a rock or island and revealing what happens there, he stops to explain it and to urge his moral lesson. Unlike Spenser, who rarely interrupts his narrative to give a personal response, Googe continuously obtrudes himself, until the allegorical object often dissolves out of view. Having detailed the shipwreck of greedy souls on the rock of Avarice, for example, he proceeds to inveigh against misers in general for ten stanzas (39–48; sigs. B5v–B6v), concluding with a vision of their discomfiture at the bar of God's judgment that is entirely unrelated to the nautical allegory. Similarly, having exhausted the possibilities of his serpent-infested island of Detraction in four or five stanzas (53–57; sigs. B7v–B8), he rails against slanderers for twenty more, recalling their notable victims from Moses through Jesus and His disciples (63–69; sigs. B8v–C1v). Although Googe no doubt congratulated himself on incorporating a certain amount of improving satire and moral pedagogy in his poem by way of these and similar digressions, in fact they cripple his rhetoric. Type satire without allegorical concretion is notoriously unfocused and flat, and Googe's capsule summaries of lore from scripture, history, and mythology are too sketchy to arouse much interest and too brief to sustain it.

When he does stretch the flimsy veil of his allegory to cover them, the satiric passages take on increased vigor. The denizens of the island of Pride, for example, turn out to be a crowd of overdressed courtiers. The women deck themselves in "scarfes and fethers . . . / With painted heare and shamelesse bared brest" (19; sig. B3); worse, the "monstrous sort of men" cinch up their waists and parade in "frisled heare like harlots of the stewes" (20; sig. B3). They all stay up nights devising fashionable costumes, but "vnderneath their garments glistering braue, / Lies mindes corrupt as rotten bones in graue" (22; sig. B3v).

The most resonant sections of the poem paint surrealistic allegorical tableaux like those found for instance in the emblem books popular during the Renaissance.[52] On the beach of Avarice "great Caskets heaped lie, / And Cofers stuft with euerie kinde of coyne" (38; sig. B5v), and the reader comes face to face with the avaricious—pale and wasted, pointlessly grasping their bane in "feeble fingars," anchored to the spot by the weight of the bags of coin that hang upon them (37; sig. B5v). The flat of Gluttony is littered with corpses and "broken Barkes" from whose holds "Great tunnes of wine" and elegant provisions have been taken and spread on "sumptuous tables" (81; sig. C3). The serving men who stand by in attendance are a series of vividly personified diseases. Characteristically, however, Googe soon drops the personification and simply catalogs maladies, prescribing abstinence as a means of subduing the flesh.

Only in the extended section on Fleshly Pleasure does he imagine an allegorical world complex enough to embody his doctrine in a consistent and continuous vision.[53] Here he could draw for events and details on the rich tradition in which his basic simile of the soul at peril on the seas of the world is finally rooted.[54] At first view, the "earthly paradyse" of pleasure seems to be an undifferentiated *locus amoenus*, with crystal cliffs, a stately forest, bright flowers, harmonious birds, and a perfumed atmosphere.[55] When a closer look, however, reveals "shalls of Mermayds swimming here and there" (105; sig. C6) around it, singing irresistible allurements, the island takes on a very specific identity. Googe retells the story of Ulysses and the Sirens in four effective stanzas that render the moral gloss without obscuring the concrete action. When, for example, he hears the Sirens' song, Ulysses cannot "restraine the affections of his minde," but calls to his deafened crew to unbind him, and "wrests and wries . . . / To vnlose himselfe, and striuing all in vayne, / He beates his head against the Mast amayne" (108; sig. C6). Since, as Don Cameron Allen puts it, Books VII–XII of Homer's poem had long been read as "the travels of Odysseus, or Everyman, as he wandered from temptation to temptation, or didactic experience to didactic experience, through the Mediterranean Sea of human life,"[56] Googe can enrich his allegory without interrupting it when he includes this material.

His account of the island of pleasure itself follows smoothly because what goes on there derives from the standard interpretation of what Circe does to Ulysses' companions.[57] Fair ladies beckon the passing ships "to enter vp the brooke," and the sailors "hoyse and hale" with all their might to "run themselues vpon this pleasure braue" (110, 112; sig. C6v). Once landed, however, they are blindfolded, led to a nearby castle through a gate inscribed, "The resting place of fleshly fond delight" (114; sig. C7), and brought before a scornful and merciless queen. At her whim, some are transformed into beasts in token of their having succumbed to animal lusts; others experience Dantesque or Petrarchist versions of the lover's hell: to stare through eyes forced open "Upon the beautie that is them denide" (116; sig. C7), to have birds rip at their hearts, or to have "Hote burning coales" closed up within their breasts (117–18; sig. C7v).[58] Nonetheless, people flock to this island, even the supposedly strong, wise, and holy. Therefore, we ought to steer away, and, when tempted by the pleasures of the flesh, "We ought to binde our wills to reason strong, / As to the Mast that beares our chiefest saile" (133; sig. D1v).[59]

By returning to his allegory in the process of expounding his moral Googe deepens the relationship between his idea and the figure used to express it, charging his exhortation with the emotional force of Ulysses' heroic self-restraint. Similarly, by generating a modicum of irony and suspense in his narration of the sequential approach, entrapment, and punishment of the sailors who put in at the harbor of Fleshly Pleasure, Googe (for once in this poem) transcends static *noun-allegory*,[60] with its simple one-to-one equations of personification or emblem to idea, and approaches the allegory of analysis and discovery that points beyond itself to a profounder truth.

Spenser used static allegory at times, as in the parade of the Seven Deadly Sins, but his account (*FQ* II. xii) of Guyon's voyage, although in many ways it recalls "The Ship of Safegarde" and its tradition, aims not to carry the hero and the reader past a set of fixed obstacles and deliver them at the pearly gates but to amplify the meaning of Guyon's destroying the Bower of Bliss within himself.[61] Googe, by contrast, tries to treat all human experience through the simple analogy of the voyage. Since he has no hero whose experiences can be given enriched significance by the allegory, the meaning of his poem is limited to what is explicit in the correspondence itself.

In his eighth eclogue, Googe had used the figure effectively on a more appropriate scale. Rosemond Tuve criticized that passage for lacking sufficient detail to meet her "criterion of sensuous vividness."[62]

The defect is even more apparent in "The Ship of Safegarde," for as Googe expands his development of the analogy the ratio of sensuous detail to abstract idea declines and the surface of the allegory, stretched to airy thinness, splits out at every seam. Indeed, Googe is at pains repeatedly to strip away any obscuring veil that may have interposed itself between his reader and the truth. The literal surface of "The Ship of Safegarde" aims only to give hortatory punch to preformulated moral admonitions. In this Googe follows rhetorical principles like those laid down by Thomas Wilson, who included allegory under his list of tropes: "An Allegorie is none other thyng, but a Metaphore vsed throughout a whole sentence, or Oration."[63] Wilson cites Heywood's *Proverbs* as examples of allegories (p. 199); although Googe's figure is not exactly proverbial, it can be expressed in as brief a form.[64] But in using it throughout his whole "oration," Googe fails to transform his comparison of man's life to an ocean voyage consistently from a simile to a metaphor. Even Wilson might have faulted him for writing merely an extended simile.

Argument by analogy is notoriously tricky, and while Googe means only to teach set doctrine through an appeal to the imaginative faculty, his rhetorical mode actually distorts his message. The concept of a ship sailing through treacherous waters toward a safe haven places a special construction on experience, ranging temptations in sequence and thus suggesting both that they may be passed and never encountered again and that to succumb to any of them results, like shipwreck, in total defeat. Ironically, a more complete realization of the vehicle of Googe's extended metaphor might have prevented these falsifications of its tenor. Both Ulysses and the Redcrosse Knight, for instance, on their allegorical (or allegorized) journeys, learn about the dangers they confront by experiencing them first hand, sometimes getting into trouble over their heads (as is inevitable for fallen man) but never sinking beyond the possibility of escape or rescue. The only protagonist in Googe's poem is the reader, whom Googe continually enjoins to see himself as the emblematic mariner. Since this shadowy second person can never actually enter the fiction and fall to any temptation—it is always *they*, the other foolish sailors, who fall, though *you may*—the dangers remain untested and the opportunity for repentance undreamt of.

In warning youthful readers away from sin, Googe may have thought it best to de-emphasize the chance for forgiveness. His decision to forego a continuous allegorical fiction in this poem may have been

influenced by his work on *The Zodiake of Life*. Palingenius too bur-
dens his allegorical frames with discursive sermonizing and invective
and seems from time to time to forget that his words are supposed to
be coming from the mouth of some fictional interlocutor. So Googe, as
if swayed by his master to place the highest value on explicit teaching,
literally leaves nothing to the imagination but sets aside his figure
whenever he deems it necessary to convey his meaning in no uncertain
terms or to include noteworthy tangential information. The result is
neither satire nor epic, but schoolbook it may be and surely is sermon.
Googe dresses up his doctrine in the threadbare rags of an epic voyage,
but, since in the eyes of humanist pedagogy the purpose of stories given
to young readers, whether Aesop or the *Aeneid*, was to teach wisdom
in a pleasant form, he tries to play the roles of bard and schoolmaster
at once. He takes us on an odyssey to marvelous islands, and he also
explicates each, providing, as Sir Thomas Elyot would have the learned
tutor do for his charges, "so moche instruction that they may take
therby some profite."[65]

It is perhaps unfair to damn "The Ship of Safegarde" for failing as
a narrative. Googe used the term "stories" in his dedication to refer
specifically to the two bits of legendary history at the back of the book.
The long poem itself he offers as a compendium of wisdom whose utility excuses the artistic defects he readily admits: "a Ship but rudely
furnished, and God knowes symply rygged, as the great haste a[n]d
small tyme enforced, wanting both strength of tymber and comlynesse
of proporcion, two euydent signes of an vnskilfull workeman" (sig.
A2v).

When he put down his pen at the end of "The Ship of Safegarde,"
Googe had written his last original poem. When he took it up again to
versify the church legends, he began the series of translations that comprised his remaining literary labor. Those works will concern us in the
next chapter. Although he apparently felt he had exhausted his stock
of strong timber for invention and lost his knack for comely disposition
in original composition, Googe approached the latter half of his career
as no unskillful craftsman of verse. Struggling with the *Zodiake* and
composing poetry of his own, if it had not purged his style of mid-
century crudities, had at least taught him some sophisticated effects.
Apart from the striking allegorical landscapes mentioned above, the
most memorable parts of "The Ship of Safegarde" are moments of
felicitous versification.[66] Even Milton might have approved of Googe's
line on the prideful, for example, who "Fall headlong downe to euer-

lasting wo" (27; sig. B4). The plight of the soul at sea in this world, "Where nought but death the fearefull eye can see," is rendered in a forceful series of parallel phrases that buffet the reader appropriately:

> Now forced with windes, now driuen backe with tide,
> Nie drownd with cares, and bet with miserie,
> Amased with mists, and wandring without light. . . . (9; sig. B2)

The preponderance of monosyllables and of heavier stresses in the phrases preceding the caesuras in each of these lines balances the half-lines against each other, while assonance and alliteration tie the beginning of each line to the end of the previous one to give a sense of unremitting or renewed pressure just where we expect a pause in the whirling rhythm. In referring to the "giltie gilted hande" (48; sig. B6v) of the avaricious, or in mentioning "Murder all embrued with bloud" (200; sig. E2), Googe sets a standard for ornate phrasing that he happily does not often live up to. Clarity and directness are his admirable goals, and he sustains a level of discourse to which colloquialisms and proverbs add vigor without disruption. It is a style well suited to the purposes—satiric, argumentative, didactic, and practical—to which it would soon be put.

CHAPTER 5

The Later Translations: Images of Life

IN his life of Sir Philip Sidney, Fulke Greville used terms like those
of "The Ship of Safegarde" to explain that his own poetry, drawing
more "upon the Images of Life, than the Images of Wit," is addressed
"to those only, that are weather-beaten in the Sea of this World, such
as having lost the sight of their Gardens, and groves, study to saile on
a right course among Rocks, and quick-sands."[1] Similarly, Googe,
especially after weathering his first trip to Ireland in 1574, chose no
longer to range through the zodiac of his own wit but to confine himself to the proven imaginings of others, notably Palingenius, to whom
he returned for the definitive *Zodiake* of 1576. Subsequently, he found
guidance through the moral and practical perils of life in three new
books he translated between 1577 and 1579. The work of this prolific
period, together with two legends from ecclesiastical history in *The
Shippe of Safegarde* (1569), a timely anti-Papist volume of 1570, and
Googe's last publication, a medical pamphlet printed in 1587, is the
concern of this final chapter.

Although he imagined translation patronized by the Muses, Googe
pursued his art according to the simplest of principles. Striving always
for a "faythfull and true translation," he aimed merely to make useful
works available in English. He rendered the texts "in some places verse
for verse, & word for worde." "In other places (where I haue not precisely obserued so strickte an order) yet," he insists, "haue I no whit
swarued from the perfect minde of the autoure."[2] His diverse translations all reflect the conviction that he could better serve his readers and
please his patrons with satiric, didactic, and practical writings than
with works of fancy, even if purged of sin. The small library he
"englished" deals with topics ranging from the miracles of a martyred
bishop to the best way to hatch duck eggs. Reading through it reinforces the notion of the universal curiosity of the Renaissance mind
and inspires admiration for the endurance and workmanship of the
translator.

I   *The Tales from Church History*

The two narratives Googe versified from "Eusebius" and included in *The Shippe of Safegarde* occupy a middle ground between translation and original composition. Googe's source was the Latin version of the *Ecclesiastical History* made by Tyrannius Rufinus around A.D. 401. Rufinus scrupled neither to revise the Greek original when it suited him nor to add details or whole incidents to the record.[3] One such passage supplies the second of Googe's stories, to be discussed below, although it appears in Book VII rather than Book IV as his headnote wrongly affirms. The first tale, "The death of S. Polycarpus, Bishop of Smyrna, and disciple to saint Iohn," comes from Book IV, Chapter 15. A comparison of Googe's version with Rufinus's, which in this case is a close rendering of the Greek,[4] will show how Googe adapts his source to suit his juvenile English audience.

Although he follows the historical narrative incident by incident, Googe suppresses some points, expands on others, and strives always to eliminate confusing issues, clarify obscure passages, heighten the drama, and drive home the moral point. To set up the conflict between "The poore afflicted Christian flocke" (1. 5) and its wolvish Roman persecutors, he provides a dozen lines (fourteeners) of prologue naturally absent from the original. His simplified version of how the eighty-six-year-old bishop was arrested slips no opportunity to evoke sympathy for the victim and hatred for the "cursed Catchpolles" (1. 41) who torment him. When, for example, Polycarp's captors hurry him down from a wagon, causing him to hurt his foot,[5] Googe has it that "they threw him headlong downe" and "hurt him verie sore" (11. 88–89).

Googe had to make other changes in the ancient story of the martyrdom of a saint to render it suitable for Tudor readers. While the source stresses the miraculous proleptic vision of fire experienced by Polycarp on the eve of his capture and the uncanny way in which his blood, coursing from a wound made by the impatient executioner's sword, extinguishes the towering flames that surround him, Googe deletes references to the bishop's "dreame" whenever he can and allows that the fire was quenched by blood only "In diuers places of the pile" (1. 205). Likewise, he totally rewrites Polycarp's final prayer in Protestant language. When God's voice booms out over the arena, it says in Rufinus's Latin, "fortis esto, Polycarpe, et viriliter age" (Mommsen, p. 343; sig. E3v), "Be strong, Polycarp, and play the man" (Lake, p. 347), but in Googe's English it says, "Be of good comfort

Polycarpe / and keepe thy conscience well" (1. 94), as the translator steers away from anything that might be misread as merely pagan heroism. While for Eusebius and Rufinus Polycarp's sainthood derives in part from the miracles that attended his death, the martyred bishop interests Googe, as an interpolated passage (11. 50–58) makes clear, almost entirely as an exemplar of steadfast resistance to temptation in face of threatened physical torment—not unlike the Protestant martyrs who went to the stake in England during his childhood. Thus the tale's theme harmonizes more fully than Googe saw fit to claim with the purport of "The Ship of Safegarde" itself.

The brief story of "A Priest of Apollo straungely conuerted" is less moralistic; it deals in irony and wonder and rounds off the book with a happily-ever-after conclusion. High in the Alps stands a temple where many repair to hear the oracles of the god. When "One Gregorie, a christian Bishop olde" (1. 10) spends a night there in his travels, the attendant priest entertains him by explaining the details of his cult. After Gregory leaves in the morning, however, he discovers that the idol has fallen silent. That night the god informs him in a dream that he cannot speak without the bishop's permission. Catching up with him on the morrow, the priest reminds Gregory of his former hospitality and the bishop expresses his gratitude by writing:

> Unto Apollo Gregorius greeting sendes,
> I giue thee leaue, do as thou didst before. (11. 81–82)

When this paper is placed on the altar, "The Idoll streight beginnes againe to prate" (1. 89), but Apollo has lost his standing with the priest, who follows Gregory, and, "falling flat" before him as he has previously done before his idol, begs to learn about the stronger God, is converted, and ultimately succeeds his patron as bishop.

Googe again follows Rufinus point for point but enriches the account with details of setting, action, and dialogue.[6] His brisk pentameter quatrains advance the narrative without interruption for sermon or satire; in concision, structure, and wit the poem maintains the highest standards of the *Eglogs, Epytaphes, and Sonettes*. It is unfortunate that Googe found these stories "tedious," as he tells his sisters-in-law in the dedication, and wrote no more. His public and satiric interests had gained the upper hand, and his next work, addressed to no less a personage than the queen, aimed less to foster virtue in the young or amuse them with stories than to enlighten the nation at large about the enemy of the day.

II   The Popish Kingdome

It is pleasant to surmise that the "learned Maister Bale" who encouraged Googe to translate Palingenius also introduced him to the congenially Protestant works of Thomas Naogeorgus or Kirchmeyer.[7] Twice an exile for his reformed beliefs and an outspoken Protestant in print, the old antiquary may well have placed in the hands of his young friend such tracts as the vehemently anti-Catholic satire *Regnum Papisticum* and a handbook for a reformed ministry called *Agriculturae Sacrae Libri Quinque*.[8] Although his translation of *The Popish Kingdome* did not appear until 1570, some seven years after Bale's death, Googe explained that he had done the two books of "The Spirituall Husbandrie" appended to give bulk to the volume "long before."[9]

Naogeorgus, a German cleric of independent mind, is primarily remembered for his Latin plays, including the intensely anti-Papist *Pammachius* (1538), whose impact was great enough to precipitate an inquisition by Bishop Gardiner when it was produced at Cambridge in 1545.[10] Apparently ill-disposed to adhere on the basis of tradition or authority to doctrines that seemed to him erroneous, Naogeorgus set himself up not only against Rome but against the Wittenberg reformers as well. The *Regnum Papisticum* rings with the sarcastic fervor of the outsider to whom everything with which he does not agree appears a conscious fraud perpetrated by men of power and evil motives. His view of the Roman church as composed entirely of knaves and fools animated by greed and fear narrows the poem's emotional range, but the oversimplification makes the work an effective piece of propaganda. It was with a sure sense of purpose that Googe chose to publish *The Popish Kingdome* in 1570, in the midst of a crisis in the conflict between England and Rome, as a study of the queen's "greatest aduersarie."

The general argument of the poem is simple: the Pope, or Antichrist, by establishing himself as the arbiter of who is saved and who is damned, has gained sway over everyone foolish enough to believe him. He uses this power to extort wealth and other worldly rewards, presiding over a hierarchy of graft and emulation through which the "lothsome poyson" (fol. 17v) of his avarice and pride seeps out into the world at large (cf. fol. 27v). Since for Naogeorgus salvation is God's free gift to all believers and cannot be earned through good works or bought from the clergy, the Pope and all his train are engaged in a

gigantic confidence racket, peddling through all their manifold rituals
and other operations something that is not theirs to sell.

The first two books survey the ranks of the clergy. The extravagance
of their claims to authority and the complex distinctions among their
titles and duties have a Lilliputian absurdity, but Naogeorgus does not
regard the Papists with any amusement: their worldly power shapes
the fate of nations; their greed strips the people of the fruits of their
labor. The third book anatomizes the main rites of the church in ironic
terms, showing how the Mass, pilgrimages, worship of relics, and the
rest are used to prey on the anxieties of the faithful.

Book Four, which has been useful to students of late medieval and
Renaissance popular customs,[11] mocks traditional holiday ceremonies.
Following his usual satiric strategy, Naogeorgus gives a deadpan, literal-minded account of symbolic rituals and semiserious or entirely
recreative revelry, viewing the old customs as ignorant superstition or
dangerous idolatry. Here his humorless tone, which was effective
enough in ridiculing "the iesture straunge . . . And shuffling vp and
downe of Clarkes" (fol. 10v) in the Mass, becomes tiresome, even when
punctured by irony. Although a concluding complaint about the religious wars and persecutions to which German Protestants were subjected and which Englishmen in 1570 had reason to fear reminds us
that the poem treats an issue of urgent seriousness, it is nonetheless
refreshing now and then to catch in a flash of energetic verse or a vivid
image a hint that the poet and his translator were not entirely immune
to the beauty of the customs they described—as in these lines on a
Christmas ceremony:

> This done, a woodden childe in clowtes is on the aultar set
> About the which both boyes and gyrles do daunce and trymly jet,
> And Carrols sing in prayse of Christ, and for to helpe them heare,
> The Organs aunswere euery verse, with sweete and solemne cheare.
>
> (fol. 45)

To establish that this is idolatrous, Naogeorgus goes on to compare it
to the "Coribants . . . vpon the mountaine Ide," who sang and beat on
brass pans to hide the crying of the newborn Jupiter from his father.
Here even the pagan parallel is charged with exotic fascination, but
the general impression of the popish kingdom conveyed by Book Four
is of a world gone mad with inane processions, frantic efforts to ward

off evil spirits, divination, dancing, drunkenness, and lechery. On Corpus Christi Day, for example, everyone parades behind a loaf of bread that is protected from the "doung" of "some mad birde" (fol. 53v) by a rich canopy; at Shrovetide the same fools "beare a torde, that on a Cushion soft they lay, / And one there is that with a flap doth keepe the flies away" (fol. 48).

As Peirce says (p. 104), *The Popish Kingdome* is better satire than the controversial pamphlets it resembles, and Googe's translation enriches it with a vigorous and colorful English idiom: the appurtenances of Roman religion are "gewgawes" and "trumperies" (fol. 9); Jesuits will be damned with other "rifraffe" (fol. 25); and unbelievers receive no grace from baptism, "though ten times in the fludde they sowsed be" (fol. 31). Although he remains close to the original, Googe caters to his public by deleting learned allusions, explaining confusing terms, and adding vivid descriptive details.[12]

The two books of "The Spirituall Husbandrie" lack the vigor and precision of the longer poem.[13] Rather than distorting and exaggerating actual men and manners in order to satirize them, Naogeorgus develops a bookish extended simile like that of "The Ship of Safegarde." Man's mind is a field; God planted seeds of grace and virtue there, but Satan sowed weeds and thistles. After the Fall, God persuaded Adam to become a good husbandman of his soul, but in subsequent generations Satan's cockles sprang up again to harm the crop. Since the Incarnation, good seeds are found in the word of God preached by Jesus and the apostles: the New Testament is "the arte of husbandrie" (fol. 65). The weeds of heresy and superstition still spring up; the rock of sin still breaks the plow. But God sends "learned labourers" (fol. 65) to till the field, spiritual husbandmen whose requisite background, constitution, and training are developed in standard humanist terms. After a full presentation of "the learnings liberall" (fol. 69) and a defense of study on the basis that its alternative is sloth, the first book ends with an attack on pride. The second begins with a similar discussion of avarice, a particular danger to the learned, whose sins are worse than those of the lewd, Naogeorgus affirms, inveighing against lust and gluttony and elegant living. Thus chastened and prepared, the learned preacher is advised to sow the seed he finds in the word of God, confining himself to scripture, especially the books of Moses, the Prophets, and the Gospels. At times his enthusiasm for the inspired parts of the Bible seems to be leading Naogeorgus toward a contempt for human learning similar to that of the "franticke Anabaptistes" (fol. 72v) he condemns: "No neede is here to vexe the minde with turning many bookes," he says (fol. 78v), expressing an attitude that may well have given his studious translator pause. But since the Holy Ghost, like many "prophane wryters" (fol. 79v), tends to be something of an allegorist, Naogeorgus would allow the preacher what help he needs to find out the hidden meaning and explain it to his flock. Book Two therefore ends with a reading list of sacred and secular works presented in the form of a plan for arranging the minister's bookshelf. The part of the treatise that Googe translated, then, forms a coherent introduction to the calling of the Protestant ministry. As a comparatively readable presentation of stock moral doctrine and some key points of Protestant theology, it provides a suitable counterweight to the invective of the longer poem. But neither work approaches the curious appeal of the two books that Googe, with seven more years of hard experience on his back, next undertook to translate.

III   The Overthrow of the Gout

In 1577 Abraham Veale issued a little book entitled *The Overthrow of the Gout / Written in Latin Verse, by Doctor Christopher Balista.* A translation of two Latin poems by Christophe Arbaleste, a physician and sometime Reformation preacher in Switzerland, the volume is dedicated by "B.G." to "his very good Frende" Richard Masters, the queen's physician.[14] Although "the verse in Latin is not very eloquent," Googe confesses himself "somthing delighted with the writer" and says he set about the work "partely for mine owne recreation" but mainly "for the benefit of diuerse my freends troubled with that disease." In this he follows his author, who several times mentions with outrage the affliction of his patient, Philip of Platea, Bishop of Sion (Sedun), Switzerland, and seems to have written the poem while working on his case.

The modern reader of the first poem in *The Overthrow of the Gout,* a rendering in 344 broken fourteeners of Balista's "In Podagram Concertatio," will note a tension between its sophisticated mock-heroic machinery and its naively confident presentation of remedy after outlandish remedy to be prepared from the herbs, spices, minerals, and animal substances that were the stock in trade of ancient pharmacology. But as Googe's other translation of 1577, the *Fovre Bookes of Husbandry,* attests, the extremes of literary refinement could coexist in the sixteenth century with the most practical information. Amusing as it may be, Balista's heroic style does not belittle his subject, but rather suggests that, to the afflicted, the battle against crippling gout is indeed a matter of epic seriousness. Balista uses elevated passages as a frame for his lists of remedies and rules for good living. His occasional digressions to recount incidents relating to the gout from classical literature or to give a short panegyric on the virtues of swine grease or "Colewort" reveal that, despite its concentration on the details of preparing and applying medication, the poem is a piece of humanistic book learning. Balista compiles all the remedies for the gout that his scholarship has been able to unearth.[15] Any one of scores of herbs or fats, applied in every conceivable fashion, should put the sufferer back on his feet in no time, but Balista seems drawn to the most nauseous preparations, and Googe makes it a point of honor to follow him without batting an eye,[16] matter-of-factly reproducing the formulae for turning goose grease, urine, bird droppings, seaweed, and "Beauers stones" into sovereign remedies, and helpfully adding alternatives or supplying idiomatic English names in the margin. A prescription for applying to the feet a poultice made from wax and the ashes of a crow that has been buried alive in horse manure is offered with characteristic confidence: it will make "the poore diseased man, / to go without a stay" (sig. Clv).

The much shorter poem (sixty-six fourteeners) that closes the volume, "A Dialogue betwixt the Gout and Cri. Balista," serves as an envoy to the whole. As before, Balista blends wit with sympathy for victims of the gout and a general Christian-humanist moralism. Gout opens the poem with a woeful lament. Like her own victims, she is stabbed with pain and can walk no faster than a tortoise. "Alas," she cries, "and shall I dye?" "Thou shalt," the poet intrudes, giving his name and announcing pompously that he is the one responsible for bringing her to the point of death (sig. C6). When Gout complains, he taxes her with having plagued virtuous men, and when she then pleads for pity, he agrees to spare her on two conditions: that she will release Bishop Philip from his torments and that she will henceforth afflict only the wicked, especially gluttons (sig. C7v).

In arguing that Googe was indeed the "B.G." who translated *The Overthrow of the Gout*, Peirce remarks that it must have appealed to his fondness for "encyclopedic trivia" (p. 168). More than that, Balista's little book gave him a chance to combine his scholarly, moral, and poetic concerns with the interest in medicine and horticulture evident elsewhere in his works to an unquestionably utilitarian purpose.

IV   *The* Fovre Bookes of Husbandry

Googe had still more to say on medicinal herbs in a long digression
interpolated into his version of the *Fovre Bookes of Husbandry* by
Conrad Heresbach. This handsomely printed prose treatise of well over
150,000 words was the most popular of Googe's books apart from the
Zodiake. It was issued three times during Googe's life (1577, 1578, and
1586), again in 1596, 1601, and 1614, and in a revised version by Gervase Markham in 1631. The esteem in which it was held is justified by
the interest, usefulness, and readability of its contents.

The original, *Rei rusticae libri quatuor,* is part of a series of works
on rural subjects composed during his retirement by Heresbach (1496–
1576), a Rhineland humanist and servant of the Duke of Cleves.[17] It
compiles the teachings of ancient and modern authorities on (as Googe
expresses it in his subheadings) "earable ground, tyllage, and pasture";
"Gardens, Orchardes, and Wooddes"; "feeding, breeding, and curing
of Cattell"; and "Poultry, Foule, Fishe, and Bees." Each book introduces one or more experts who respond to the inquiries of their companions by discoursing at large on the excellence and practical details
of their occupations.

At the start Heresbach portrays in Cono a learned gentleman like
himself whose daily activities include study and prayer and who can
defend in good set terms his withdrawal from court to country, so that
when he cites Varro, Theophrastus, Cato, Columella, Dioscorides, and
Laurentius in a single breath (sigs. D3–D3v) or quotes at length in
verse from Vergil or Horace, it seems no less probable than when he
explains the best arrangement of farm buildings by leading his interlocutor on a tour of his estate or names the tools in his toolshed as he
points to them one by one. But when in Book Three four herdsmen
demonstrate similar learning as they pass a holiday in conversation
under a tree by preference to the tavern or when Melisseus in Book
Four regales his friends by quoting long passages on bee-keeping from
the *Georgics,* it becomes clear that verisimilitude did not interest Heresbach and that he used the dialogue form primarily as a way to orga-
nize the voluminous information he had gleaned from his studies. Having decided to devote himself to cultivating his lands, like a true
humanist Heresbach read everything he could find on the subject and
set forth his knowledge in a pleasant form for the benefit of others.

One of his beneficiaries was Googe, who had himself gone to farm-

ing, or at least gardening, at Kingston in Kent after his first trip to
Ireland and who was looking forward eagerly to the day when he could
take possession of his father's lands in Lincolnshire.[18] For the "further
profite and pleasure" of his English readers, Googe added what he
could from "myne owne readinges and obseruations, ioyned with the
experience of sundry my freendes." Although he admits that some of
what he takes by way of Heresbach from "the olde auncient hus-
bandes, as well Greekes as Latines," (sig. (iij)) concerns plants foreign
to England, he is confident that they can be naturalized—even the
vine, which used to be grown in England and should be reintroduced
for the benefit of the realm.

Googe devotes a full page to listing the authorities on which he and
Heresbach have drawn. After "The Byble, and Doctors of the
Churche," he gives fifty-nine Greek and Latin writers, and then, in a
separate group, he names eighteen Englishmen, some of whom are
authors, some his neighbors and acquaintances.[19] "My freend Wylliam
Prat, very skilful in these matters," contributes a recipe for preparing
asparagus (sig. G6v); from "Maister Ihon Franklin of Chart in Kent,
who was in his life time a skilfull husband, and a good housekeeper,"
comes a treatment for ailing horses (sig. S8). "Maister Fytzherbert, a
Gentleman of Northamptonshyre, who was the fyrst that attempted to
wrighte of husbandry in England," is quoted *in extenso* for a way to
cure a "Sheepe that haue a woorme in his foote" (sig. S7v).[20] Such
interpolations, along with more personal asides like the eulogy of his
grandmother (sig. X7v) or the praise of Sir Thomas Challoner's horse-
warden (sig. Q2) mentioned above (pp. 19, 21), may be slightly
unnerving to a reader who recalls that he is supposed to be hearing the
words of Chenoboscus or Hippocomus as written by Heresbach, not
the first-person discourse of Barnabe Googe. That Googe felt it proper
to "increase" Heresbach in this fashion and at the same time could
insist in the preface to the *Gout* that one ought not to be "to curious
in an other mans woork" reflects the peculiar nature of the body of
lore contained in the *Husbandry*, which grew and evolved from redaction to redaction, from Heresbach and his sources through Googe and
his to Markham's revision and beyond, as if with a life of its own.

Googe is nonetheless quite right in the epistle to the reader when he
judges that, despite his contributions, it would not be just, "as diuers in
the like case haue done," to issue the book under his own name.
Indeed, he adds only one new passage of more than a page in length,
the discussion of medicinal herbs (sigs. +5v–Aa1v) included "because

maister Hersbach hath shewed you before in his Garden many good hearbes, and yet not whereto they serue" (sig. +6). Googe cites various authorites, including Cardanus, Mathiolus, and Hieronymus Tragus,[21] but his personal enthusiasm for actually growing, collecting, and distilling herbs is apparent. He tells of receiving angellica seeds from "that vertuous and godly Lady, the Lady Golding in Kent" (sig. +6v), reports that cardiaca grows "plentifully in Surry" (sig. +8v) while "Pennygrasse" is found "by the shadowy Ditches, about great Peckham in Kent" (sig. +7v), and insists "that you doo not distill them, as the vnskilful doo," in metal vessels, but only in glass (sig. Aa1). Earlier, in the third book, he illustrates a discussion of black ellebore root, "once brought vnto me . . . from Darndal in Sussex, . . ." with a picture of the plant, "for your better knowledge." But Googe like Heresbach feels more comfortable relying on authority than on experience. He ends paraphrasing Mathiolus (sigs. R4–R4v), and even the picture, although not a direct copy, appears to be imitated closely from one given by Tragus.[22]

The main effect of Googe's interpolations is to add a little English flavor to the foreign text. He completes a survey of cheeses with some discriminating commentary on the product of various regions of England, capped by an epigram from "our English Martial," John Heywood (sig. T3v); he endorses Heresbach's opinion of the voraciousness of sows by recalling one that devoured a child in Sussex, "to the pitifull discomfort of the parent" (sig. T6); and notes in the margin English applications of the methods described. In the epistle dedicatory to his 1631 revision, Gervase Markham complained that Googe had not gone far enough in adapting the book to English conditions: the work was "taught to speake English by a learned Gentleman Master *Googe*, who was so faithful to the first Author that it became an vtter stranger to our Climate" (sigs. A2–A2v). Googe's version won the critical esteem of William Webbe, however, who remarked in 1586 that Googe "deserued much commendation, as well for hys faythfull compyling and learned increasing the noble worke, as for hys wytty translation of a good part of the *Georgickes* of *Virgill* into English verse."[23]

The terms of Webbe's praise suggest the reasons for the book's success and the nature of Googe's accomplishment in teaching it to speak English. He delivered to his countrymen a practical handbook on agriculture—so used, as annotations in some surviving copies attest— that was also a learned treatise, a commendation of the simple country life, and a tour de force of literary art. In the view of agricultural history, the *Husbandry* stands out for having brought to England advanced methods practiced in the Low Countries.[24] For the student of literature its significance lies in its successful combination of so many seemingly disparate elements.

Although it may have diminished Googe's reputation not to print his translations from the *Georgics* separately, they were for him an integral part of their larger context. Peirce, who has studied them along with the other snippets of verse scattered through the *Husbandry* (pp. 118–35), shows that Googe neither offers a word-for-word literal gloss on his originals nor attempts to reduplicate their more subtle refinements in English. Rather, he subdues them to the purpose at hand, striving to make accessible to the reader the information they contain.

With Vergil's bees, that information involves also a notation of the commendable industry and orderliness of the hive that allows Heresbach and Googe to sustain the sequence of moral asides that drop with ease and regularity from their pens. The *Husbandry* opens with a version of the familiar debate over the relative merits of service to the prince and otiose retirement, attended as always by attacks on the corruption of the times. In his dedication to Sir William Fitzwilliams, then leaving active service in Ireland, Googe seconds the preference for the country life, and near the end of Book One he adds a bitter aside about the unruly depredations of upstarts like those he attacks in "Egloga tertia," including an epigram from Claudian and an English proverb to enforce the point.

Like Balista, Heresbach tried to make his treatise not only profitable but pleasant as well, and his translator followed his lead. Vivid descriptive passages and occasional poems, jokes, and stories help the reader along. Heresbach recalls how the sound a walnut tree makes before it falls once frightened people in Antandro out of the baths and into the street (sig. O4v); he describes a gooseliver he saw at the Diet of Worms that weighed a full four pounds (sig. X4v); he even repeats a tall tale— "when I was Embassador in England, it was told me by men of good credite"—of a tree in Scotland whose fruit, if it falls into the sea, turns into ducks (sig. X5v). Googe, as we have seen, contributes some anecdotes of his own and renders Heresbach's poised Latin into a zesty colloquial English. Once, he feels compelled to disagree with his author in vehement terms. After patiently following Heresbach's detailed account of the behavior and usefulness of cats as long as he can, Googe finally breaks off, ignoring further material on their excretory habits, the loyalty of castrated toms, and so on, and exclaims, "For my part I would rather counsell you to destroy your Rattes and Mise with Traps, Banes, or Weesels: for besides the sluttishnesse & lothsomenesse of the Catte (you know what she layes in the Malt heape) she is most daungerous and pernicious among children, as I mee self haue had good experience" (sig. U4v).[25]

The charm of the *Husbandry* lies in its hospitality to all kinds of topics, from the most private opinion to the broadest public concern, and to all levels of tone, from levity through matter-of-fact exposition to solemn piety. That the principles of unity and decorum never seem to be outraged may result from the book's total disregard for both, and yet the final impression it leaves on the reader is one of coherence, reliability, and pleasurable interest.

V   The Prouerbes *of Santillana*

The last of the series of translations Googe published during the later 1570s promises more than its predecessors, but it delivers less. Like the *Husbandry, The Prouerbes of the noble and woorthy souldier Sir Iames Lopes de Mendoza Marques of Santillana, with the Paraphrase of D. Peter Diaz of Toledo*, is a collective effort: the wisdom of the ages and of personal experience versified by an aristocrat, expounded by his learned chaplain, and presented in English with a modest contribution here and there by the translator. Don Iñigo Lopez de Mendoza, Primer Marqués de Santillana (1398–1458), was one of the most important literary and political figures of his time in Castile.[26] A good poet himself, in native and medieval modes as well as in the new Italian manner, he patronized humanistic learning by assembling a large library and harboring a number of scholars in his court, one of whom was Doctor Pedro Diaz.[27] King Juan II requested the *Proverbios* for the edification of his son, Prince Enrique. The work was completed in 1437 and immediately became popular, circulating first in manuscript and then in print—twenty-nine editions before the end of the sixteenth century.[28] The translation did not enjoy a similar success, but its contents have interest as a reflection of English literary taste after two decades of Elizabethan rule and as an index of Googe's concerns and abilities at the end of his literary career.

Moreover, the book contains a prose life of Santillana that represents the first and perhaps the only publication in English of a work by Fernando del Pulgar, author of the *Libro de los claros varones de Castilla* (Toledo, 1486).[29] Googe found Pulgar's portrait of the Marqués appended unsigned to the text of the *Proverbios* he evidently used, a combined edition in Spanish of "Seneca's" proverbs and those of Santillana, both glossed by Diaz, printed in 1552.[30] His version of Pulgar's Spanish is close enough to account for the observation of one reader unaware of its source that "the Elizabethan English curiously suggests the Spanish of Santillana's own day."[31]

As Pulgar portrayed him, Santillana must have appealed to Googe not only for his exemplary learning and virtue, but also for a more personal reason: like Googe, Santillana had to fight to regain his patrimony.[32] No doubt the parallel was not lost on Cecil, to whom Googe dedicated *The Prouerbes* in the confidence that both its author and its doctrine would be welcome to his moralistic patron.

During the 1570s, works of moral didacticism found increasing favor in the eyes of the established leaders of the realm, while amatory lyrics and tales fell ever more under suspicion as conducive to vice. For Googe, the Marqués of Santillana fills the role of the moralizing Gnomaticus in Gascoigne's *The Glasse of Government* (1575), setting down the precepts of virtue for a promising member of the younger generation. Santillana claimed in his "Prólogo" to be speaking as a father to his son after the manner of Solomon in the biblical proverbs,[33] and he stresses in the text as well the superior wisdom, virtue, and reliability of age over youth.[34] As the father of growing sons himself, Googe perhaps approved the doctrine as much as he knew Cecil would, but a good part of his delight in the work must have arisen from the learning displayed in the gloss.

In proverb 12 (fol. 27v)[35] Santillana declares that the reason for study is to aid in the reprehension of sin—just what the book seeks straightforwardly to do. The hybrid text combines the qualities of the medieval didactic lyric and the humanist treatise, surrounding Santillana's concise and allusive aphorisms[36] with a rich embroidery of explications, analogues, and authorities. Despite the intervening glosses, the proverbs are not entirely separable but form the stanzas of a continuous moral poem. Like many, it lacks an adequate structure.[37] Diaz frequently points out relationships between stanzas, but aside from ending with age and death, the Marqués seems merely to have set down all the things Prince Enrique would need to know in the order they happened to come to mind. Drawing on the ancients, the scriptures, the church fathers, and medieval and modern writers,[38] he dispenses the familiar tenets of Christian stoicism at tiresome length.

The most serious weakness of *The Prouerbes* is the absence of an authorial personality. Only when he descends from morals to manners to expound a more worldly kind of wisdom does the Marqués escape bookishness. "Flee Taletellers," the reader is advised (7); "be comformable to the time" (20); and pick a wife not for her money but for her tractability (43, 44). Once, he even approaches the rueful self-irony that distinguishes some of Googe's own short poems, in proverb 87, which concludes:

> Ofte haue I found my selfe by speache
>   in thrall and trouble brought:
> But neuer yet for keeping of
>   my toung, I suffred ought.

The *Proverbios* have been praised for their mnemonic qualities,[39] but in Googe's version few are easily remembered—or even apprehended. In rendering Santillana's stanza of four lines of eight syllables alternating with four of four as two fourteener couplets, Googe had to use about forty-five words to say what the Marqués said in twenty-five. Thus he threw away concision, one of the main virtues of the *Proverbios* and, when present, of his own style, and because of the plain abstraction of the originals he could not replace it with the imagery, wit (*The Prouerbes* are entirely humorless, as Peirce observes, p. 141), concretion, and fresh diction that enliven his other translations. Free from the need to fill up empty iambs, Googe generally did better with the prose gloss of Diaz. He gives lively versions of exemplary narratives about Coriolanus, Tarquin, Damon and Pithias, and others, and, when Diaz here and there generates a glimmer of irony, Googe propagates it eagerly: "aske of the Ladie *Venus,* howe chaunce shee hath so colde entertainement in the poore labourers houses, where you shall seldome or neuer see any of them goe mad for loue" (fol. 62; cf. 1494, sigs. F7–F7v).

Remarkably, Googe found little to disagree with in the book, although it was the work of two Catholic Spaniards. He translates some reverent verses on the Blessed Virgin without blinking (47) and endorses with notes in the margin congenial teachings on gluttony and lechery (fol. 54v) and on scripture reading (fol. 30).[40] Only once does any anti-Spanish feeling come to the surface. Diaz argues that, although one should not maintain by alms anybody capable of working, exception should be made for an able-bodied person so nobly born that "he cannot abase himself to any vile occupation." "A right Spanish stomacke," Googe remarks (fol. 81).

Googe made two small additions to *The Prouerbes*. The first, a cynical note next to a story about how Caesar himself went to court to represent a common soldier who had formerly served him, is the more biographically suggestive: "Hard for a souldier in these daies to finde a *Caesar*" (fol. 12). The second has more literary interest. In the gloss on proverb 84, the first four lines of Petrarch's sonnet "Ceasare poi che'l traditor d'Egitto" are quoted and then paraphrased in Spanish prose. Googe translates them into competent pentameter:

> Caesar, when as the false Egyptian had
> Presented him with worthie Pōpeys hed,
> Hiding his ioy with coloured coūtnance sad,
> His fained teares foorthwith, they say, he shed. (fol. 99v)

By naming Pompey (Petrarch does not), Googe clarifies the application of the passage to the argument Diaz is developing, and his fourth line is a manifest improvement over a literal version of the original: " . . . wept with his eyes, externally, as it is written."[41]

The modicum of skill here displayed implies that, although *The Prouerbes* is a disappointing finale for his most productive period as a translator,[42] Googe's powers remained intact. By no means the best work of its original authors,[43] the book was written and translated into English for the specific purpose of moral pedagogy. Such works have little appeal for a sophisticated audience: the *Proverbios*, treasured by the Spanish people for many years, was also subjected to parody,[44] and Shakespeare's treatment of Polonius suggests the knowledgeable later Elizabethan's attitude toward the whole tradition. It is unfortunate but should not be surprising that Googe catered to a much less up-to-date taste in the works of his middle years than he did in the forward-looking poetry of his youth.

VI   *The* Terra Sigillata

Googe's last publication, *The Wonderfull and strange effect and vertues of a new Terra Sigillata lately found out in Germanie, With the right order of the applying and administring of it: being oftentimes tried and experienced by Andreas Bertholdus of Oschatz in Misnia*,[45] has little or no literary value. Its curious contents and Googe's attitude toward them reveal that, then as now, men were frightened enough of death and disease to place their faith in pseudoscientific wonder drugs and that there was no lack of pious charlatans to prey on them. In tones of solemn patriotism and restrained enthusiasm, Googe dedicates to Doctors Masters and Baylie, physicians to the queen, his credulous translation of the Latin brochure that came with some medicine sent him by Hugh Morgan, "her Maiesties Apothecarie."[46]

After listing thirteen different types of illness, from poisoning to the plague, that are cured by the "greace of the Sunne" (p. 15) he prepares from the slag of a gold mine near his home, Bertholdus gives detailed instructions for its use. Surely this miraculous remedy is one of God's blessings on his favored nation, and it is more patriotic and economical to use the German product than similar substances imported at great expense from the land of the Turk: plenty is available for purchase at the printer's office in Frankfurt. The doubtful are referred to the testimonials of certain noblemen and officials printed at the back of the book. These documents, duly notarized or sealed patent, describe public experiments in which the medicine prevented death by poisoning— once for a group of dogs (the deaths of a control group are described in detail), once for a prisoner named Wendel Thumblart, who escaped hanging by volunteering for the test.

In his prefatory epistle, Googe adds that the medicine has been found "most effectuall in sundrie dreadfull and daungerous diseases" by his friend "M. Doctor *Hector,* Nunnes and diuerse others of your learned Colledge in *London*" (sig. A3v). His strictly practical concern is reflected in the inelegant but clear style of the translation, through which the outlines of Bertholdus's Latin syntax and, in the testimonials, a deeper layer of legal German may be discerned. Finally seated on his patrimonial lands in Lincolnshire, Googe found reason to go to press only this once, in quest of favor not from Cecil, whose help he no longer needed, but from physicians, the only men whose worldly aid, at the age of forty-seven, he now required.

Whatever their accomplishments in moral enlightenment, service to the nation, personal self-definition, or artistic beauty, most of Googe's publications had the coordinate purpose of gaining the good will of those able to better his condition. It is a tribute to his integrity, however, that he never translated anything whose value he doubted would serve his readers' best interests as well as his own. Though he did not live directly on the proceeds from his books, Googe must be considered more a professional writer than a courtly amateur. That writing was nonetheless never his primary occupation as it was for Spenser or Shakespeare may partially account for the limitations of his works.

Still, the level of competence he maintained in most of the translations discussed in this chapter might have gained Googe a more prominent station in literary history if he had expended his efforts on works of classic rank. Even had he been able to free himself from the hesitations of self-doubt, however, from the peculiar perspective of his generation, the Renaissance works he chose to "english" appeared to have unquestioned value—and Googe probably regarded the *Aeneid* as the property of Phaer and the *Metamorphoses*, which Golding rattled out in verse decidedly inferior to Googe's own in 1567, as tainted with paganism and vice. Although he hoped for lasting fame mainly as a translator, the *Zodiake*, *The Popish Kingdome*, and the *Husbandry* did not carry his name beyond his time. Nevertheless, they do lend weight and substance to the clear and living voice that still speaks in Googe's original poems—not least in "To the Translation of Pallingen," his most serious meditation on "the labour swete" of his chosen craft.

Notes and References

Chapter One

1. Barnabe Googe, "The Preface" to *The First thre Bokes of . . . the Zodyake of lyfe*, by Marcellus Palingenius, trans. Googe (London: Iohn Tisdale, for Rafe Newberye, 1560), sigs. °5v–°7v. The various editions of this translation are hereinafter referred to as *Zodiake*, followed by the appropriate date.

2. Barnabe Googe, *Eglogs [,] Epytaphes, and Sonettes* (London: Thomas Colwell, for Raffe Newbery, 1563), sigs. I1v–I2. Hereinafter referred to as *Eglogs, Epytaphes, and Sonettes* or *EE&S*. Because of irregularities in the signatures of this volume, subsequent citations refer to the pages as numbered in the facsimile edition by Frank B. Fieler (Gainesville, Fla.: Scholars' Facsimiles & Reprints, 1968), although the text is transcribed from an eletrostatic copy of the original in the Huntington Library, since the facsimile contains several false emendations.

3. Googe was noted and some of his works were listed by Anthony à Wood in 1691–92, although he is partly confused with one of his descendants. See *Fasti Oxoniensis*, part I, col. 310–11, in Anthony à Wood, *Athenae Oxoniensis*, ed. Philip Bliss (London: F. C. and J. Rivington et al., 1813–20; rpt. New York: Johnson Reprint Corp., 1967). Material on Googe was subsequently printed in such works as John Strype's *Life and Acts of Matthew Parker* (Oxford: Clarendon Press, 1821; orig. pub., 1711), pp. 286–89; Thomas Tanner's *Bibliotheca Britanno-Hibernia* (London: G. Bowyer, 1748; rpt. Tucson: Audax Press, 1963), pp. 332–33; Samuel Egerton Brydges's *Censura Literaria* (London: Longman, Hurst, Rees, and Orme, 1806), II, 170, 206–208, 211–12; his *Restituta* (London: Longman, Hurst, Rees, Orme, and Brown, 1816), III, 35; IV, 307–11, 359–65; and Charles Henry Cooper and Thompson Cooper, *Athenae Cantabrigiensis* (Cambridge: Deighton, Bell & Co., 1858; rpt. Farnborough, Hants.: Gregg Press, 1967), II, 39–40. Brydges (*Restituta*, I: 364) ridicules Googe's hope for immortality even as he helps to fulfill it.

4. See Thomas Warton, *History of English Poetry*, ed. W. Carew Hazlitt (London: Reeves and Turner, 1871), IV, 203, 323–31. Warton's *History* was originally published in 1774–81; more material on Googe is added by later editors in the 1871 edition. See also Edward Phillips, *Theatrum Poetarum Anglicanorum* (Canterbury: Simmons and Kirkby, 1800), pp. 123–26; Edward Farr, ed., *Select Poetry Chiefly Devotional of the Reign of Queen*

119

Elizabeth (Cambridge: Cambridge Univ. Press, 1845), pp. xxv, xxxvi, 388, 391–92; W. J. Courthope, *A History of English Poetry* (London: Macmillan, 1897), II, 153–58; Harold H. Child, "The New English Poetry," in *Cambridge History of English Literature* (Cambridge: Cambridge Univ. Press, 1909), III, 187–215, pp. 208–10; George Saintsbury, *A Short History of English Literature* (London: Macmillan, 1929), p. 254; C. F. Tucker Brooke, "The Renaissance," in *A Literary History of England*, ed. A. C. Baugh (New York: Appleton-Century-Crofts, 1948), pp. 391–92; and C. S. Lewis, *English Literature in the Sixteenth Century, Excluding Drama* (Oxford: Clarendon Press, 1954), pp. 258–59.

5. John Payne Collier, *The Poetical Decameron* (Edinburgh: Constable, 1820), p. 121.

6. Hyder E. Rollins and Herschel Baker, *The Renaissance in England* (Boston: D. C. Heath and Co., 1954), p. 286. They have a similar opinion of George Turbervile, who is "the Rosencrantz to Googe's Guildenstern" (p. 291). Googe might not seem to academic wits quite so much like a comic-strip character if his name were still pronounced, as it apparently was in his own time, to rhyme with *coach*.

7. Don Cameron Allen, *Image and Meaning: Metaphoric Traditions in Renaissance Poetry* (Baltimore: Johns Hopkins Press, 1960), p. 12.

8. *The Renaissance in England*, p. 286.

9. Edward Arber, ed., *Eglogs, Epytaphes, and Sonettes*, by Barnabe Googe (Westminster: Constable, 1871, 1895), pp. 15–16.

10. R. C. Hope, ed., *Reprint of The Popish Kingdome . . . 1570* (London: [privately printed], 1880). He includes a readable but derivative account of Googe's life.

11. John Erskine, *The Elizabethan Lyric: A Study* (New York: Columbia Univ. Press, 1905), pp. 98–101.

12. Yvor Winters, "The Sixteenth-Century Lyric in England," *Poetry: A Magazine of Verse* LIII (1939): 258–72, 320–35; LIV (1939): 35–51, rpt. with revisions in Winters, *Forms of Discovery* ([Chicago]: Alan Swallow, 1967), pp. 1–52.

13. See Alan Stephens, ed., *Selected Poems of Barnabe Googe* (Denver: Alan Swallow, 1961); Douglas L. Peterson, *The English Lyric from Wyatt to Donne* (Princeton: Princeton Univ. Press, 1967), pp. 134–45; John Williams, ed., *English Renaissance Poetry* (Garden City, N.Y.: Anchor, 1963; rpt. New York: Norton, 1974); and William Tydeman, ed., *English Poetry, 1400–1580* (New York: Barnes & Noble, 1970), pp. 137–39, 250–51.

14. Apart from glowing commendations from his cousin Alexander Neville and his coadjutor L. Blundeston printed with his poems, Googe's own verse is praised by William Webbe in *A Discourse of English Poetrie* (London: Iohn Charlewood for Robert Walley, 1586), sig. C4, and seems to be included in the remarks of Richard Robinson, who in a dream sees Googe crowned with laurel and seated on Helicon along with Skelton, Lydgate, and others near the end of *The rewarde of Wickednesse* (London: William Williamson,

1573/4), sig. Q2v, as well as in the salute given him by Gabriel Harvey in *Pierces Supererogation* (1593), in Harvey's *Works*, ed. A. B. Grosart (London: [privately printed], 1884), II, 290.

15. See Jasper Heywood's preface to his translation of *The second tragedie of Seneca entituled Thyestes* (London, 1560), sigs. °7v–°8 (quoted by Arber, pp. 5–6); T. B.'s preface to John Studley's translation of *The eyght tragedie of Seneca, entituled Agamemnon* (London: T. Colwell, 1566), sig. A1; Roger Ascham, *The Schoolmaster (1570)*, ed. Lawrence V. Ryan (Ithaca, N.Y.: Cornell University Press), pp. 145–46; Arthur Hall's dedicatory epistle to his *Ten Books of Homers Iliades, translated out of French* (London: Ralph Newberie, 1581); and Francis Meres, *Palladis Tamia (1598)*, ed. Don Cameron Allen (New York: Scholars' Facsimiles & Reprints, 1938), fol. 285v.

16. See C. H. Conley, *The First English Translators of the Classics* (New Haven: Yale Univ. Press, 1927; rpt. Port Washington, N.Y.: Kennikat Press, 1967).

17. The precise nature of the kinship between Googe and Cecil has never been specified, and my efforts to trace it through the genealogical tables published by the Harleian Society and others have yielded only the impression that the connection was a matter of broad family alliances rather than a close and definite blood or marital tie between two individuals. One actual link is perhaps the exception that proves the rule: the third husband of Googe's maternal grandmother, Sir James Hales, was the grandson of Robert Atwater; Atwater's daughter Mary was the mother of a Robert Honeywood (whose son Thomas Googe called "cousin"); Robert Honeywood's wife Elizabeth Browne was the granddaughter of Sir William Fitzwilliams, Lord Deputy to Ireland and patron of Googe, who was the brother-in-law of Sir Anthony Cooke, father of Mildred, second wife of Sir William Cecil.

18. By *sonnet*, of course, Googe meant any short poem not otherwise designated. There are, however, two right sonnets in his collection, overlooked by some because they were printed in lines broken after the second foot. See Hoyt H. Hudson, "Sonnets by Barnabe Googe," *PMLA* LXVIII (1933): 293–94, and P. N. U. Harting, "The 'Sonettes' of Barnabe Googe," *English Studies* XI (1929): 100–102. A third sonnet has been observed in Googe's translation of a passage from Columella in the *Fovre Bookes of Husbandry* (1577), sig. G3v, by Brooke Peirce in "Barnabe Googe: Poet and Translator," Diss. Harvard, 1954, p. 122.

19. See Googe's standard defense of poetry in the preface "To the vertuous and frendely Reader," *Zodiake*, 1565, sigs.(‡)2–(‡)4.

20. This holds true for, among others, George Turbervile, Geoffrey Fenton, and Thomas Howell. George Gascoigne seems to have been following it before his death in 1577. Cf. the related generational model discussed in Richard Helgerson's *Elizabethan Prodigals* (Berkeley: Univ. of California Press, 1976), esp. pp. 4–15.

21. My account of Googe's life relies mainly on the biographical chapter in Peirce, which is grounded on extensive original research and which

supersedes the incomplete and sometimes erroneous tradition enshrined in the *DNB*. My other biographical sources are cited as used; Peirce, used throughout, is not always cited.

22. No direct record of his birth survives. The information in *Lincolnshire Pedigrees*, ed. A. R. Maddison (London: Harleian Society, 1902–06), II, 408, that he was fifteen years and eleven months old on the death of his father in 1557 indicates 1541. The record of his mother's death on July 24, 1540 (Peirce, p. 6, n. 3), however, argues for 1540, as does Googe's autograph in a copy of Sir Thomas Challoner's *De Republica Anglorum* giving his age as thirty-nine in 1579 (see *Fasti Oxoniensis*, part I, col. 311, in *Athenae Oxoniensis*, ed. Bliss). Finally, his two dedications of *Zodiake*, 1560, are dated March 10 and March 28, presumably of 1560, so that his description of himself as *in his twentieth year* again yields 1540.

23. The family name is often spelled so, or *Gooche*, or *Gooch*, but in his published works Barnabe always prints it *Googe*.

24. See Peirce, pp. 6–7, and the references he cites.

25. On the Kentish connections, see Peirce, pp. 8–10.

26. Conrad Heresbach, *Fovre Bookes of Husbandry*, trans. Barnabe Googe (London: Richard Watkins, 1577), sigs. X7v–X8; see also sigs. C4v, +6v, and +7v. This work is hereinafter referred to as *Husbandry*.

27. See Richard C. Barnett, *Place, Profit, and Power: A Study of the Servants of William Cecil, Elizabethan Statesman*, James Sprunt Studies in History and Political Science, Vol. 51 (Chapel Hill: Univ. of North Carolina Press, 1969), pp. 66–67; Peirce, p. 302; William Pinkerton, "Barnabe Googe," *Notes & Queries*, 3rd ser., III (1863), 141–43, 181–84, 241–43, 301–302, 361–62, p. 302; and "Barnabe Googe to Lord Burghley," 26 September 1586, in Historical Manuscripts Commission, *Calendar of the Manuscripts of . . . the Marquis of Salisbury* (London: for H. M. Stationery Office, by Eyre and Spottiswoode, 1888), II, 522.

28. Thomas Wilson, *The Arte of Rhetorique (1553)*, ed. Robert Hood Bowers (Gainesville, Fla.: Scholars' Facsimiles & Reprints, 1962), p. 143.

29. B. W. Beckingsale, *Burghley: Tudor Statesman, 1520–1598* (London: Macmillan, 1967), p. 89.

30. See Barnett, pp. 65–67. On Robert Goche and Cecil, see n. 24 above.

31. His relative and patron Sir William Fitzwilliams, for example, was "a contributor to the afflicted professors of the gospel in the time of Queen Mary" (*General Index to the Historical and Biographical Works of John Strype, A.M.* [Oxford: Clarendon Press, 1828], I, 285). He addressed poems to the former exiles Alexander Nowell and John Bale. His patrimonial lands, indeed, had been confiscated from the church under Henry VIII. See W. Morton, "Goche of Alvingham Abbey (Priory?)," *Lincolnshire Notes & Queries* IV (1894): 109–12; and Agnes Cuming, "Some Documents Connected with Alvingham Priory," *The Lincolnshire Magazine* III: 2 (1936): 38–40.

32. On Hales's imprisonment, recantation, and suicide, see John Strype, *Ecclesiastical Memorials* (Oxford: Clarendon Press, 1822), III, i, pp. 274–76; on Grimald, see L. R. Merrill, *The Life and Poems of Nicholas Grimald* (New Haven: Yale University Press, 1925), pp. 36ff., and Louise Imogen Guiney, *Recusant Poets* (New York: Sheed & Ward, 1939), pp. 82–92.

33. John Venn and J. A. Venn, *Alumni Cantabrigiensis, Part I* (Cambridge: Cambridge Univ. Press, 1922), II, 231.

34. See H. C. Porter, *Reformation and Reaction in Tudor Cambridge* (Cambridge: Cambridge Univ. Press, 1958), esp. pp. 72–73, and Strype, *Ecclesiastical Memorials*, III, i, p. 570.

35. Googe to Burghley, 11 March 1583, quoted by Pinkerton, p. 243.

36. The attribution to Googe of this poem, which is signed "B. G.," was first suggested in James Kennedy et al., *Dictionary of Anonymous and Pseudonymous English Literature (Samuel Halkett and John Laing)* (Edinburgh: Oliver and Boyd, 1926–34), VI, 300. It is tentatively confirmed by Peirce (pp. 149–54) on the basis of circumstance and style. The thematic issues stressed here add further credence to the attribution. It appears in *A Briefe Treatise . . . of the Popes vsurped Primacye*, trans. Thomas Gressop (London: Henry Sutton for Rafe Newbery, 1560), sig. A7v.

37. And apparently the misdirected scorn of some who took it for a work of astrology. See Peirce, pp. 14–17.

38. For a discussion of this expedition, see John Garrett Underhill, *Spanish Literature in the England of the Tudors* (New York: Macmillan, 1899), pp. 238–45. See also Peirce, pp. 18–21.

39. See *Calendar of State Papers, Foreign (Elizabeth)*, V, 9–10, 74 (Items 19, 153, 155). Underhill is mistaken in declaring that Googe brought home parcels for Sir Thomas Chamberlain, for the license to export them had expired when he left. See ibid., pp. 40–41, 74 (Items 76, 155).

40. The entry appears halfway through those for 22 July 1562 to 22 July 1563. See *A Transcript of the Registers of the Company of Stationers; 1554–1640 A.D.*, ed. Edward Arber (London: Privately Printed, 1875), vol. I, fol. 88v.

41. See Edwin Haviland Miller, *The Professional Writer in Elizabethan England* (Cambridge, Mass.: Harvard Univ. Press, 1959), pp. 142–49. Blundeston (or "Blunderston," as some writers insist on calling him) became a successful lawyer. See *Alumni Cantabrigiensis, Part I*, I, 170; John Peile, *Biographical Register of Christ's College, 1505–1905*, ed. Venn (Cambridge: Cambridge Univ. Press, 1910–13), I, 57; and Peirce, p. 21.

42. See Underhill, pp. 240–42; T. P. Harrison, Jr., "Googe's *Eglogs* and Montemayor's *Diana*," *University of Texas Studies in English* V (1925): 68–78; and Judith M. Kennedy, ed., *A Critical Edition of Yong's Translation of George of Montemayor's "Diana" and Gil Polo's "Enamoured Diana"* (Oxford: Clarendon Press, 1968), pp. liv–lv.

43. See Strype, *Life of Parker*, pp. 286–89.

44. Archbishop Parker to Sir William Cecil, 20 November 1563, *Correspondence of Matthew Parker,* ed. John Bruce and Thomas Thomason Perowne (Cambridge: Cambridge Univ. Press, 1853), p. 198; cf. Arber, pp. 12–13.

45. Googe to George and Edward Darrell, 26 October 1563, in Arber, p. 12.

46. See Peirce, pp. 23–24. The marriage date is given by Peile, I, 56.

47. See Peirce, p. 29. Among the nine children, eight survived to adulthood. The eldest, Mathew, born in 1566, inherited Googe's lands in Lincolnshire; Robert became a Fellow of All Souls' College, Oxford; and Barnaby, LL.D., was Master of Magdalene College, Cambridge, and Chancellor of the Diocese of Exon. See Maddison, II, 408–409. He may also have been the "Dr. Bar. Gooch" who for a time held a patent under the Plymouth Company for lands in New England. See Samuel Peters, *General History of Connecticut (1781),* ed. S. J. McCormick (New York: Appleton, 1877), p. 13.

48. On September 16, 1566, Googe sold a manor and some land in Lincolnshire to Mary's brother George. See *Calendar of Patent Rolls, Elizabeth I* III (1563–1566): 404 (Item 2261).

49. G. B., *A newe Booke called the Shippe of safegarde* (London: W. Seres, 1569). Hereinafter referred to as *The Shippe of Safegarde.*

50. Thomas Naogeorgus, *The Popish Kingdome, or reigne of Antichrist,* trans. Barnabe Googe (London: Henrie Denham for Richarde Watkins, 1570), hereinafter referred to as *The Popish Kingdome.*

51. Barnett, p. 66.

52. *Calendar of Patent Rolls, Elizabeth I* V (1569–1572): 440 (Item 3092).

53. He is recorded as a server at a reception for the French Commissioners in 1581 (Barnett, pp. 66–67; Beckingsale, p. 150), and in a letter to Burghley from Ireland in 1582 he regrets having to break off his "daily attendance upon your lordship" (Historical MSS. Commission, *Salisbury,* part II, p. 522).

54. Iñigo Lopes de Mendoza, Marqués of Santillana, *The Prouerbes . . . with the Paraphrase of D. Peter Diaz of Toledo* (London: Richarde Watkins, 1579). Hereinafter referred to as *The Prouerbes.*

55. With the exception of the one in the *Salisbury MSS.* cited above, they are cataloged in the *Calendar of State Papers, Ireland (1574–1585).* The bulk have been reprinted or summarized by Pinkerton, from whose texts I quote, citing parenthetically. Additional background is included in the fulsome account by M. D. O'Sullivan, "Barnabe Googe, Provost-Marshall of Connaught, 1582–1585," *Journal of the Galway Archaeological and Historical Society* XVIII (1938): 1–39. For a reprint of a map Googe drew of the town of Galway, see her study, "The Fortification of Galway in the Sixteenth and Early Seventeenth Centuries," *Journal of the Galway Archaeological and Historical Society* XVI (1934): 1–47, facing p. 9. Another sketch by Googe, the miniature portrait of an Irish chieftain, has been reprinted by

Eleanor Hull, *A History of Ireland and Her People to the Close of the Tudor Period* (London: George G. Harrap, 1926), p. 358. Peirce recounts Googe's Irish experiences on pp. 32–37, 44–50.

56. Googe to Burghley, 26 September 1582, Historical MSS. Commission, *Salisbury*, part II, p. 522.

57. The legitimacy of his claim to the job is explored by O'Sullivan, "Barnabe Googe," *Journal of the Galway Archaeological and Historical Society* XVIII (1938): 22, 29ff., 36.

58. Historical Manuscripts Commission, *The Manuscripts of . . . the Duke of Rutland* (London: for H. M. Stationery Office, by Eyre and Spottiswoode, 1888), I, 219.

59. Andreas Bertholdus, *The Wonderfull and strange effect and vertues of a new Terra Sigillata lately found out in Germanie*, trans. B. G. (London: Robert Robinson for Richard Watkins, 1587), hereinafter referred to as *Terra Sigillata*.

60. The tradition that he translated "Aristotle's Tables of the Ten Categories" appears to have arisen from an error by Thomas Warton. See Warton, ed. Hazlitt, IV, 330–31.

61. Warton, IV, 328. Gordon Braden offers an interesting discussion of the problems and possibilities of the fourteener in "Golding's Ovid," part one of his *The Classics and English Renaissance Poetry* (New Haven: Yale Univ. Press, 1978), pp. 22–35.

62. As has been pointed out by John Thompson, *The Founding of English Metre* (New York: Columbia Univ. Press, 1961), pp. 66–68.

63. See George Gascoigne, "Certayne Notes of Instruction Concerning the Making of Verse or Ryme in English" (1575), in *English Literary Criticism: The Renaissance*, ed. O. B. Hardison, Jr. (New York: Appleton-Century-Crofts, 1963).

64. The pentameter lines in *EE&S* are likewise split after the second foot, but the only result is confusion to the reader. In quoting, I have followed the printed text in the case of long lines, but have indicated the break in pentameters only by inserting a virgule (/).

65. Winters, *Poetry* LIII, (1939): 264–65; Winters, *Forms of Discovery*, pp. 19–20. See also Stephens, pp. 15–16.

66. A detailed discussion of this issue may be found in Richard Jacob Panofsky, "A Descriptive Study of English Mid-Tudor Short Poetry," Diss. University of California, Santa Barbara, 1975. I am indebted to Panofsky throughout my book.

67. See Veré L. Rubel, *Poetic Diction in the English Renaissance* (New York: Modern Language Assoc. of America, 1941), pp. 134–36, 171–74. See also Peirce, pp. 263–68.

68. Robert Pinsky, *The Situation of Poetry* (Princeton: Princeton Univ. Press, 1976), p. 4.

Chapter Two

1. Rosemond Tuve's introduction to her facsimile edition of the *Zodiake* (New York: Scholars' Facsimiles & Reprints, 1947) provides a fine account of the original and the translation; I am indebted to it throughout the present chapter. Tuve's text is copied from 1576, and she conveniently reprints prefatory material from other editions. Her commentary is hereinafter referred to as "Tuve, intro."

2. In the appendix to the *Zodiake* of 1561, sig. U2.

3. *Zodiake*, 1565, sig. °7. On the epic tone, see also Peirce, p. 94.

4. As Peirce suggests, pp. 12–13. Heywood lists Googe among other translators at work at the Inns and Temples. See Chapter 1, n. 15, above.

5. See Mario Emilio Cosenza, *Biographical and Bibliographical Dictionary of the Italian Humanists* (Boston: G. K. Hall, 1962), III, 2551–53; V, 1302–1303. The date of the first appearance of the *Zodiacus vitae* is given variously from 1528 to 1534. See Tuve, intro., p. v, and Francis R. Johnson, *Astronomical Thought in Renaissance England* (Baltimore: John Hopkins Press, 1937), pp. 69, 145–46, 193. See also Foster Watson, *The "Zodiacus Vitae" of Marcellus Palingenius Stellatus: An Old School-Book* (London: Philip Wellby, 1908), which offers a summary of the text, including liberal quotations from the Latin and Googe's translation, along with useful commentary and a compendium of previous scholarship. Watson gives evidence of the poem's reputation in England and Europe, pp. 72–85. Benedetto Croce gives an account of the poem's philosophy and style in "Lo 'Zodiacus Vitae' del Palingenio," in his *Poeti e Scrittori del Pieno e del Tardo Rinascimento* (Bari: Guis. Laterza & Figli, 1952), III, 84–92.

I have consulted *Marcelli Palingenii Stellati Poetae doctissimi Zodiacus vitae: hoc est. De hominis vita, studio, ac moribus optime instituendis, Libri XII* (London: Henry Bynneman, 1572), hereinafter referred to as *Zodiacus*.

6. For schools where the *Zodiacus vitae* was prescribed by statute during the sixteenth and seventeenth centuries, see Foster Watson, *The English Grammar Schools to 1660: Their Curriculum and Practice* (Cambridge: Cambridge Univ. Press, 1908), p. 379; Watson, *Zodiacus*, pp. 5–8; and John Erskine Hankins, *Shakespeare's Derived Imagery* (Lawrence: Univ. of Kansas Press, 1953), p. 13. It is worthy of note that all the statutes postdate the first and second editions of Googe's translation.

7. See Tuve, intro., pp. xv–xxiv.

8. *Zodiake*, 1565, sig. °7v. See Watson, *Zodiacus*, pp. 11–15. Tuve examines other possible reasons for his being considered a heretic (intro., pp. xxii–xxiv).

9. *Zodiake*, 1561, sigs. O1v–O2; pp. 75–76. My references to the text of the *Zodiake* are to the signatures of the 1560, 1561, and 1565 editions (which remain the same from edition to edition), and to the page numbers of the

1576 edition and the identical 1588 reprint. The first citation gives the source of the lines as quoted.

10. Sig. A2v, quoted by Peirce, p. 128, n. 2. My point here arises from a suggestion made by Peirce, pp. 127–32.

11. "Quae gerit hic clypeus Probitatis fulgida signa / Vendicat et celebrat Gogaea clara domus," says the inscription beneath it.

12. Trans. Barnabe Googe (London: Ihon Tisdale, for Rafe Newbery, 1561).

13. Peirce, p. 18, n. 2.

14. The acrostic and a new epigram by Duke, and longer poems by Edward Dering and G. Chaterton.

15. Trans. Barnabe Googe (London: Henry Denham, for Rafe Newberye, 1565).

16. By David Bell, who helpfully translates it into Latin. He also offers another in Latin, as do Christopher Carlile and Jacob Itzuert; the poems from 1561 by Chaterton and Duke are retained, but Dering's is dropped. See Peirce, pp. 16–17.

17. Trans. Barnabe Googe (London: Raufe Newberie, 1576); the 1588 reprint (London: Robert Robinson) is identical.

18. See for example Tuve, intro., pp. ix–x. Peirce (pp. 73–78) grants the poem a measure of unity, thanks to its consistent moral intent, to its astronomical pattern, and its general progress of concerns from human to divine. Walter Gorn Old, in "The Astrological Aspect of The Zodiac of Life," Appendix C of Watson, *Zodiacus*, pp. 86–92, argues that the subject matter of each book corresponds to concerns associated with each astrological sign, reflecting the cycle of human life. Watson notes (pp. 12–14) that in the palace at Ferrara, Palingenius could have observed a similarly constructed series of twelve frescoes.

19. Tuve, intro., pp. ix, xxi.

20. Johnson, pp. 69, 145–49.

21. Two interesting treatments of this problem and some of its literary ramifications are Helgerson, *Elizabethan Prodigals*, and G. K. Hunter, *John Lyly: The Humanist as Courtier* (Cambridge, Mass.: Harvard Univ. Press, 1962), esp. Chapter 1.

22. Sig. A3; p. 2. The Latin reads "multa & diuersa" (*Zodiacus*, p. 11). I quote throughout entirely from Googe's faithful translation, using the 1565 edition.

23. It is she who accompanies him in this book, not Arete, as Googe mistakenly notes in the margin in 1576, p. 107.

24. See Ascham, ed. Ryan, pp. 145–46; Webbe, sig. C4; and Meres, ed. Allen, pp. 285–86.

25. Tuve, intro., p. v; Hankins, p. 12; Johnson, p. 146, who cites G. C. Moore Smith, *Gabriel Harvey's Marginalia* (Stratford-upon-Avon: Shakespeare Head Press, 1913), pp. 161–64, 231. Richard F. Kennedy has called to

my attention the quotation of a long passage on marriage from "Leo" in Googe's translation by John Parinchef, *An extracte of examples, apothegmes, and histories* (London: H. Bynneman for H. Toie, [1572]), sigs. M4v–M7.

26. In two short paragraphs, Tuve ticks off parallels in eight English and two foreign writers (intro., pp. xvi–xvii).

27. See Josephine Waters Bennett, "Spenser's Garden of Adonis," *PMLA* XLVII (1932): 46–80. Bennett makes no case for direct influence of Palingenius on Spenser, but stresses their common Christian-platonism.

28. See Rosemond Tuve, "A Mediaeval Commonplace in Spenser's Cosmology," *Studies in Philology* XXX (1933): 133–47, pp. 143–44.

29. Rosemond Tuve, "Spenser and the *Zodiake of Life*," *Journal of English and Germanic Philology* XXXIV (1935): 1–19. To the parallels she notes it might be added that the description of the grove occupied by Voluptuousness also resembles Spenser's account of the Wandering Wood in Book I, into which Redcrosse and Una, to the accompaniment of "the birdes sweet harmony" (I, 1. 8; cf. *Zodiake*, "the birdes full swetely syng," sig. F1) are "with pleasure forward led" (I. 1. 8) down "alleies wide" (cf. *Zodiake*, "alleyes long," sig. F2) past a catalog of trees that could have been suggested by that of Palingenius, which names almost all of Spenser's trees, and more besides (sigs. E8v–F2; pp. 29–30).

30. In *The Analogy of "The Faerie Queene"* (Princeton: Princeton Univ. Press, 1976), p. 41, James Nohrnberg suggests an intriguing link when he remarks that Spenser's Prince Arthur resembles Hercules, that Hercules's labors were often explained as a solar myth, and that Palingenius set a precedent for organizing a long poem according to the signs of the zodiac through which the sun passes. See also Old, "Astrological Aspect," in Watson, *Zodiacus*, p. 86, and n. 18 above. It should be added that the title page of Googe's 1576 and 1588 editions contains the phrase "in twelue seuerall labours" and that the *Zodiacus vitae*, dedicated by its author to Duke Ercole II d'Este of Ferrara, frequently mentions the legendary namesake of its patron. In "Gemini" his labors are summarized by Arete, who stresses that his submission to a woman led to his humiliating confinement at woman's work in woman's clothing, just as with Spenser's other avatar of Hercules, Artegal, in Book V. Cf. Watson's description of the zodiac of frescoes at Ferrara, *Zodiacus*, pp. 12–13.

31. F. F. Covington, "Biographical Notes on Spenser," *Modern Philology* XXII (1924–25): 65–66, suggests that Googe and Spenser may have met in Ireland. Discussion of Spenser's use of Palingenius continues. See the report of a paper read at the Warburg Institute in 1979 by Ian McFarlane in *Spenser Newsletter* XI (Winter, 1980), 13–14 (Item 80.16).

32. See note 6 above. That Shakespeare probably used the *Zodiacus vitae* had previously been suggested by many scholars. See T. W. Baldwin, *William Shakspere's "Small Latine & Lesse Greeke"* (Urbana: Univ. of Illinois Press, 1944), I, 652–80, which surveys earlier references. Also see Josephine

Waters Bennett, "Jaques' Seven Ages," *Shakespeare Association Bulletin* XXVIII (1943): 168–74. Hankins acknowledges, includes, and supersedes these studies and also a 1938 University of Illinois Master's thesis by Charles Byford Garrigus. See also T. W. Baldwin, *On the Literary Genetics of Shakspere's Poems & Sonnets* (Urbana: Univ. of Illinois Press, 1950), pp. 17, 25–26, 52–55, 72.

33. Hankins, pp. 14–15.

34. See, for example, Hankins, pp. 119–20.

35. See Hankins, pp. 267ff., 131–33, 140.

36. See Hankins, pp. 145, 197–98, and 197–207 passim.

37. In this connection, it is significant that Hankins finds many parallels to the *Zodiake* in the speeches of the misanthropic Timon of Athens, who intends to abandon human society in order to escape the evils of the world. See Hankins, pp. 159–78.

38. Peirce notes several instances in passing, mostly of proverbs (see pp. 211, 213, 337, 380). Others are noted below in the present study.

39. Cf. Peirce, p. 300, who credits Palingenius with fostering the "inordinate fondness for abstraction and allegorical satire" that in his view weakens the eighth eclogue.

40. The characterization of Palingenius's style is supported by Foster Watson, *English Grammar Schools*, p. 379. See also Watson, *Zodiacus*, pp. 7–8. For early Elizabethan ideals of style, see Panofsky, "Mid-Tudor Short Poetry." See also his introduction to *"Epitaphes, Epigrams, Songs and Sonets" (1567) and "Epitaphes and Sonnettes" (1576) by George Turberville* (Delmar, N.Y.: Scholars' Facsimiles & Reprints, 1977).

41. See Tuve, intro., pp. xiv–xv.

Chapter Three

1. There are thirty-five in *EE&S*. Googe also wrote five other short poems, not counting short translated works: "Let rankour not you rule," discussed above, pp. 20–21, three poems in the 1560 and 1561 editions of the *Zodiake*, and a verse prelude to *The Shippe of Safegarde*.

2. See Peirce, p. 62.

3. The term is quoted from Panofsky, p. 21, who surveys this body of writing in detail.

4. Lewis, *English Literature in the Sixteenth Century*, esp. pp. 64–65, 222–71.

5. Winters, "The Sixteenth-Century Lyric in England." See Chapter 1, 4n. 12, above. Winters's 1955 review of Lewis is reprinted in his book *The Function of Criticism* (Denver: Alan Swallow, 1957), pp. 190–200.

6. Peterson, *The English Lyric from Wyatt to Donne*. Stephens traces out a similar thesis in the introduction to his *Selected Poems of Barnabe*

Googe, especially stressing the influence of Nicholas Grimald on Googe. I am indebted to both of these studies. Winters's influence is also evident in Williams, ed., *English Renaissance Poetry*.

7. Peterson, pp. 142, 145.

8. G. K. Hunter, "Drab and Golden Lyrics of the Renaissance," in *Forms of Lyric*, ed. Reuben A. Brower (New York: Columbia Univ. Press, 1970), pp. 1–18.

9. Hunter, pp. 8, 10.

10. Hunter, p. 17.

11. See Panofsky, pp. 4–40; Hoyt Hopewell Hudson, *The Epigram in the English Renaissance* (Princeton: Princeton Univ. Press, 1947), esp. pp. 145ff.; Baldwin, *Small Latine*, esp. II, 1–416; and Watson, *English Grammar Schools*.

12. The ensuing discussions concentrate on structure and intent and usually do not notice Googe's ornaments of style. His rhetorical figures of words and thought are frequently named by Peirce in the course of his remarks on the poems.

13. On these exercises and their relation to poetry, see Hudson, pp. 145 ff., and Panofsky, pp. 108ff.

14. In citing the short poems from *EE&S*, I refer only to the page on which a poem begins in Fieler's facsimile, here p. 125. These references are hereafter included in the text.

15. See Wilson, *Arte of Rhetorique*, ed. Bowers, p. 143.

16. But see Peirce, pp. 378–80, for a slightly different estimate of the poem. For the proverbial eel's tail, see Morris Palmer Tilley, *A Dictionary of Proverbs in England in the Sixteenth and Seventeenth Centuries* (Ann Arbor: Univ. of Michigan Press, 1950), pp. 182, 313.

17. Winters, *Forms of Discovery*, p. 3.

18. Throughout this study I refer to *Tottel's Miscellany (1557–1587)*, 2 vols., ed. Hyder Edward Rollins, 2nd ed. (Cambridge, Mass.: Harvard Univ. Press, 1965).

19. Turbervile, *Epitaphes, Epigrams, Songs and Sonets* (London: Henry Denham, 1567), fols. 124–124v. See Peirce's further remarks, pp. 356–57.

20. As Stephens calls it, p. 16.

21. Peterson, p. 137.

22. Winters, *Forms of Discovery*, pp. 19–20.

23. See *The Foundacion of Rhetorike (1563)*, by Richard Rainolde, ed. Francis R. Johnson (New York: Scholars' Facsimiles & Reprints, 1945), fol. 53v.

24. See for example *Tottel's Miscellany*, No. 296, or *The Paradise of Dainty Devices (1576–1606)*, ed. Hyder Edward Rollins (Cambridge, Mass.: Harvard Univ. Press, 1927), No. 21. Googe naturally also found the idea in Palingenius, as Hankins shows (*Shakespeare's Derived Imagery*, pp. 170–71). See *Zodiacus*, p. 52.

25. Panofsky, Appendix Two, pp. 210–14, compiles a number of previous observations. Hankins finds analogues in the *Zodiake, Timon,* and *The Passionate Pilgrim (Shakespeare's Derived Imagery,* pp. 50, 52, 55, 56, 170–74). Milton uses terms similar to Googe's in *Samson Agonistes:* " . . . in prosperous days / They swarm, but in adverse withdraw their head / Not to be found, though sought" (11. 191–93). In a recent college textbook, John Hollander prints Googe's poem with Billie Holiday's "God Bless the Child" to show that some ideas never fade. See *Literature as Experience,* ed. Irving Howe et al. (New York: Harcourt Brace Jovanovitch, 1979), pp. 372–74.

26. John Heywood, *Three hundred Epigrammes, vpon three hundred prouerbes,* No. 247, in *John Heywood's "Works" and Miscellaneous Short Poems,* ed. Burton A. Milligan, Illinois Studies in Language and Literature, Vol. 41 (Urbana: Univ. of Illinois Press, 1956), p. 190.

27. Among several pious treatments ("Golde corrupteth," "The vanite of riches"), Thomas Howell included in *The Arbor of Amitie* (London: Henry Denham, 1568) one celebration "Of Golde" (fol. 23v), but his tone is wistful, his mood envious—he would settle, he concludes, for a little "white siluer cleere."

28. See Stephens, p. 18.

29. "To Maister Googes fansie that begins Giue Monie mee take friendship who so list," *Epitaphes, Epigrams, Songs and Sonets,* fols. 115–115v. See Panofsky, pp. 131–33.

30. See A. L. Bennett, "The Principal Rhetorical Conventions in the Renaissance Personal Elegy," *Studies in Philology* LI (1954): 107–26; and Panofsky, pp. 89–92.

31. See Miller, *Professional Writer,* pp. 225–31.

32. A good example is Turbervile's "Vpon the death of the aforenamed Dame Elizabeth Arhundle of Cornewall," *Epitaphes, Epigrams, Songs and Sonets,* fols. 56–59.

33. Wilson, ed. Bowers, p. 87; pointed out by Peterson in the course of his fine appreciation of this poem, pp. 142–43.

34. Baldwin, *Small Latine,* I, 5–7.

35. Leicester Bradner apparently missed the joke—or didn't like it—when he remarked of Googe, "His muse might well stand amazed, for the worst thing Edwards ever wrote does not descend to the puerility of this effort." *The Life and Poems of Richard Edwards* (New Haven: Yale Univ. Press, 1927), p. 18.

36. Peterson, pp. 139–41, shows to what extent these two poems *do* employ rhetorical techniques.

37. Peirce identifies the battle as that usually called the battle of Pinkie (1547) and suggests another possible influence, Challoner's Latin poem on Shelley. See pp. 66, 323–25.

38. Peirce (p. 66) shows that the poem refers to the effort to put down Ket's rebellion at Norwich in 1549.

39. See Panofsky, pp. 127–36.

40. Wyatt, Tottel's *Miscellany*, No. 126, 1. 14.

41. See Rainolde, ed. Johnson, p. iv, fol. 16v. Googe most likely did not know Rainolde directly, but rather some parallel or intermediate descendant of Rainolde's ultimate source, Aphthonius.

42. Wilson, ed. Bowers, p. 81.

43. Peirce notes its sonnetlike qualities, p. 329.

44. See Panofsky, p. 139, for a similar view of "To Edwarde Cobham."

45. Stephens, pp. 15–16.

46. See Stephens, p. 16, whose version of Cicero I quote.

47. Noted by Stephens, p. 16.

48. Peirce calls these poems the "travel group" (p. 361) and relates them to Wyatt's poem and other possible sources, pp. 371–75.

49. Turbervile, for example. See my essay, "George Turbervile and the Problem of Passion," *Journal of English and Germanic Philology* LXIX (1970): 631–49. Panofsky surveys standard mid-Tudor practice in love poetry, pp. 149–95.

50. Pointed out by Judith M. Kennedy, pp. liv–lv. Her description of Googe's poem as "a fairly close translation" is somewhat misleading: Googe retains most of Montemayor's images in sequence, but he sets them forth to a new purpose in entirely different sentences and verse. He neither translates nor imitates Montemayor, but merely recycles his conceits. Cf. "Cansado está de oirme el claro río" in Jorge de Montemayor, *Los Siete Libros de la Diana*, ed. Enrique Morena Báez (Madrid: Real Academia Española, 1955), pp. 74–76; and Bartholomew Yong's true if slightly expanded translation in Kennedy's edition, pp. 54–55.

51. *Epitaphes, Epigrams, Songs and Sonets*, fol. 8v.

52. The presumed original of these lines has not been identified.

53. Wyatt's "How the louer perisheth in his delight, as the flie in the fire" (Tottel, No. 47), after Petrarch, is similar, but the idea could be found everywhere. See Leonard Forster, *The Icy Fire: Five Studies in European Petrarchism* (Cambridge: Cambridge Univ. Press, 1969), pp. x, 131ff.

54. This song is not in Tottel, but appears in the Egerton MS. 2711. See Wyatt, *Collected Poems*, ed. Joost Daalder (London: Oxford Univ. Press, 1975), p. 18. The similarity to Googe's poem is pointed out by Peirce, pp. 350–51.

55. The lines mean, *and a place where they (the ladies) care as much for your advances as did the master in Aesop for his ass that thought to gain his favor by imitating his lap dog.* Googe uses "passe" in the obsolete sense of "to care or to reck" (*OED*, Pass, verb intransitive, x, sense 23), as he also does in his sixth eclogue (p. 57). The fable appears in Caxton's Aesop, I. 17. See *Caxton's Aesop*, ed. R. T. Lenaghan (Cambridge, Mass.: Harvard Univ. Press, 1967), pp. 85–86.

56. This game was as old as the Roman Lupercalia and seems to have been

played at all levels of English society through the last century. See William Hone, *The Every-Day Book* (London: T. Tegg, 1827; rpt. Detroit: Gale Research Co., 1967), I, 222; and T. F. Thistleton-Dyer, *British Popular Customs* (London: George Bell and Sons, 1876; rpt. Detroit: Singing Tree Press, 1968), pp. 98–99. Cf. Turbervile's "Of the choise of his Valentine," *Epitaphes, Epigrams, Songs and Sonets*, fol. 119. See also Sheidley, *Journal of English and Germanic Philology* LXIX (1970): 644.

57. See Peterson, pp. 137–40.

58. In "The Ship of Safegarde" (st. 171), Googe notes that to give a woman God's rightful place in one's heart is a form of idolatry.

59. Both Stephens (p. 20) and Peterson (pp. 141–42) have singled out this poem for special comment. Peirce aptly remarks that it "is really a 'bread-and-butter' letter in verse" (p. 361).

60. On Elizabethan attitudes toward poetry as a calling, see Richard Helgerson, "The New Poet Presents Himself: Spenser and the Idea of a Literary Career," *PMLA* XCIII (1978): 893–911.

Chapter Four

1. Cf. those of Petrarch. See *Petrarch's Lyric Poems*, ed. and trans. Robert M. Durling (Cambridge, Mass.: Harvard Univ. Press, 1976), Nos. 1, 364, 365.

2. *Epitaphes, Epigrams, Songs and Sonets*, sigs. °6–°6v. See Sheidley, *Journal of English and Germanic Philology* LXIX (1970): 631–49.

3. See James J. Scanlon, "Sidney's *Astrophil and Stella:* 'See what it is to love' Sensually!" *Studies in English Literature* XVI (1976): 65–74.

4. The term is used of Wyatt by J. W. Lever, *The Elizabethan Love Sonnet* (London: Methuen, 1956), p. 31.

5. See Panofsky, p. 88 and passim.

6. Whose adaptations of Mantuan and Aenius Sylvius Googe apparently did not know. See Beatrice White, ed., *The Eclogues of Alexander Barclay* (London: Early English Text Society, 1928), p. lxi.

7. See for example Courthope, II, 153–58; W. W. Greg, *Pastoral Poetry and Pastoral Drama* (London: A. H. Bullen, 1906), pp. 80–84; Edwin Greenlaw, "The Shepheards Calender," *PMLA* XXVI (1911): 419–51; Harrison, *University of Texas Studies in English* V (1925): 68–78; Rubel, pp. 134–36; and Underhill, pp. 239–46.

8. Paul E. Parnell, "Barnabe Googe: A Puritan in Arcadia," *Journal of English and Germanic Philology* LX (1961): 273–81. Peirce had developed a cogent analysis in a long chapter of his unpublished dissertation in 1954 (pp. 215–312), noting sources and analogues. I am indebted to both these discussions.

9. Parnell, pp. 273, 281.

10. Ibid., p. 274.

11. Ibid.

12. For an Englishman of Googe's era, the pastoral eclogue was most familiar in the works of Baptista Mantuanus, or Baptista Spagnolo of Mantua (1448–1516), whose nine eclogues were prescribed at St. Paul's in 1518 and published in a popular English version by Turbervile in 1567. Mantuan offered a compendium of Christian-humanist doctrine and an example of a respected pagan form (see Michael Murrin, "Mantuan and the English Eclogue," Diss. Yale, 1965). The similarity between Googe and Mantuan has been repeatedly observed by literary historians. In his introduction to the facsimile edition of Turbervile's version (New York: Scholars' Facsimiles & Reprints, 1937), Douglas Bush remarks that Googe took Mantuan as the "general model" for his eclogues. Greg hardly grants Googe the dignity of imitating Mantuan when he characterizes most of the eclogues as "Mantuan adjusted" to the conditions of England (p. 81). Frank Kermode is somewhat misleading in the notes to his collection *English Pastoral Poetry from the Beginnings to Marvell* (London: George G. Harrap & Co., 1952), p. 242, when he states that Googe "exactly imitates Mantuan," for W. P. Mustard, editor of *The Eclogues of Baptista Mantuanus* (Baltimore: Johns Hopkins Press, 1911), having examined Googe carefully for traces of Mantuan, can find only two instances approaching translation, and these echoes are partial at best (see p. 50). Googe does not follow Mantuan closely in language, plot, or structure, but he does find in Mantuan a generic sanction for the subject matter and techniques out of which he builds his eclogues—which Peirce substantiates by noting many parallels, pp. 235–36, 250, 260–63, 272–73, 280, 283–84, 298–99, 306–307, 311. For further comparisons between Googe and Mantuan, see below in the present study, pp. 81–82.

13. Helen Cooper, *Pastoral: Medieval into Renaissance* (Totowa, N.J.: Rowman and Littlefield, 1977). Cooper shows that Mantuan was a major channel through which both the rustic-realistic *bergerie* and the moral-satirical-allegorical eclogue of the Middle Ages were conveyed to Renaissance writers in the north (pp. 108–11). She understands Googe's "Eglogs" as an unsuccessful attempt "to apply the moral outlook of the medieval tradition" (p. 125) to new Renaissance pastoral themes opened by Sannazaro's *Arcadia*, "which gave Europe a model of abstracted love-melancholy played out in a pastoral world of the imagination" (p. 100). Cooper's point holds in a sense for three of Googe's eclogues, but of course Googe does not wish to use the romantic themes, only to parody and reject them. See also Murrin, Diss., pp. 118–21.

14. William Empson, *Some Versions of Pastoral* (London: Chatto & Windus, 1950), p. 23. See also Kermode, pp. 13–19.

15. The unity of Googe's "Eglogs" and their similarity to *The Shepheardes Calender* were pointed out by Greg (pp. 84, 91) and Greenlaw (*PMLA* XXVI [1911]: 426–27). See also Peirce, p. 232.

16. Quotations from the "Eglogs" are designated by the number of the eclogue in roman, the line numbers in arabic, and the page number in Fieler's facsimile.

17. See Peirce, pp. 251–52. He notes subsequent analogues, pp. 254–56.

18. See Panofsky (pp. 165–68) for an account of Dametas's soliloquy as "a simplified deliberative oration," "school rhetoric applied to the painting of a picture of deep despair." Out of such resources, however, Googe builds a sufficiently dramatic exemplum for his homily. Dametas's absurdity is evident and presented in such a way as to make us laugh at him rather than cry with him. He is a cousin of the hopelessly deluded speaker of "Ons musynge as I sat."

19. Parnell calls this passage a "digression from private to public morality" (p. 277), while Peirce argues (p. 227) that Googe's rejection of the worldly values of the town, "most apparent" in this eclogue, "also underlies nearly all the others."

20. Parnell makes this gloss and suggests Lord Chancellor Stephen Gardiner for the upstart Coridon (p. 276). Timothy Cook, however, has suggested that the Coridon who speaks represents Barnabe Riche and the upstart his thus repudiated kinsman Richard Rich, Lord Chancellor, 1548–1551. See "Who Were Barnabe Googe's Two Coridons?" *Notes & Queries* n.s. XXIV (1977): 497–99.

21. Peirce suggests affinities with "vision-narratives" such as those in *The Mirror for Magistrates* (p. 270); Murrin finds a precedent in Boccaccio's fifth eclogue (Diss., p. 120).

22. See Harrison, *University of Texas Studies in English* V (1925): 68–78. See also *Montemayor's Diana*, ed. Kennedy, pp. liv, 10–32, 83–103.

23. See Murrin, Diss., pp. 118–19, for a similar argument.

24. Peirce, pp. 286–93. Googe's indebtedness to Garcilaso was pointed out by Underhill, p. 242. See *The Works of Garcilasso De La Vega*, trans J. H. Wiffen (London: Hurst, Robinson and Co., 1823), p. 205.

25. Peirce sees the mark of Palingenius here again (pp. 300, 306).

26. Rosemond Tuve faults this *allegoria* for having too little detail to enforce its meaning. Unlike the description of "Exces" in "Cupido Conquered" she goes on to praise, this passage makes an intellectual rather than a visceral appeal. See *Elizabethan and Metaphysical Imagery* (Chicago: Univ. of Chicago Press, 1947), pp. 107–108. See also the present study, below, p. 86.

27. Murrin (Diss., pp. 90–95) finds an ironic reversal in the self-evident folly of Amyntas's rustic mourners.

28. New York: Oxford Univ. Press, 1958 (orig. pub. 1936), p. 257. Earle Broadus Fowler, in *Spenser and the Courts of Love* (Menasha, Wis.: Collegiate Press, 1921), tabulates the outstanding conventions of the genre. "Cupido Conquered" fulfills them almost without exception.

29. Lewis, *Allegory*, p. 157. That Googe knew the *Roman* is clear from

his quotation of thirty-six lines of the Chaucerian version in *The Shippe of Safegarde*. See below, p. 93.

30. In the prefatory epistle to his collection he asks his readers "to beare with the vnpleasaunt forme of my to hastely fynyshed Dreame, the greater part wherof with lytle aduyse I lately ended, bycause the beginnyng of it, as a senseles head separated frō the body was gyuen with the rest to be prynted." It comprises 388 broken fourteeners.

31. See Geoffrey Chaucer, *The Works, 1532, with Supplementary Material from the Editions of 1542, 1561, 1598, and 1602*, ed. D. S. Brewer (Ilkely, Yorks.: Scolar Press, 1969, rpt. 1974), and *Chaucerian and Other Pieces*, ed. Walter W. Skeat (London: Oxford Univ. Press, 1897). A parallel visionary tradition was likewise sustained by editions of *Piers Plowman* in 1550 and 1551.

32. See David William Foster, *The Marques of Santillana*, Twayne's World Authors Series 154 (New York: Twayne, 1971), pp. 48ff.; A. D. Deyermond, *A Literary History of Spain: The Middle Ages* (London: Ernest Benn, 1971), pp. 183–84; and Chandler Rathfon Post, *Mediaeval Spanish Allegory* (Cambridge, Mass.: Harvard Univ. Press, 1915; rpt. Westport, Conn.: Greenwood Press, 1974), pp. 206–14.

33. See A. C. Spearing, *Medieval Dream-Poetry* (Cambridge: Cambridge Univ. Press, 1976), for an enlightening discussion. The quotation is from p. 6.

34. See J. Huizinga, *The Waning of the Middle Ages* (Garden City, N.Y.: Anchor, 1954), p. 271.

35. In citing "Cupido Conquered," I refer to line numbers, and the page numbers in Fieler's facsimile.

36. Thus Lewis, *Allegory*, pp. 125–29; but see Spearing, p. 27, for a different interpretation.

37. There is a general similarity between Googe's castle of Diana and its inhabitants in "Cupido Conquered" and the ornamentation and frescoes of the Temple of Diana in Book Four of Montemayor's romance. See *Diana*, ed. Kennedy, pp. 139–43, and liv.

38. For a brief discussion of Googe's poem as part of a tradition that treats struggles by Anteros figures against the savage Eros of Ovid's *Amores* I, ii, 19–28, see Don Cameron Allen, *Image and Meaning*, pp. 1–19.

39. *Prudentius*, ed. H. J. Thomson, Loeb Classical Library (Cambridge, Mass.: Harvard Univ. Press, 1949), I, 40–108.

40. This view is held by Fieler, pp. xix–xx.

41. Lewis, *Allegory*, p. 166.

42. Spearing views the poem as a study of the poetic vocation, pp. 202–11.

43. See Peter J. Houle, *The English Morality and Related Drama: A Bibliographical Survey* (Hamden, Conn.: Archon Books, 1972), p. xii.

44. *Written by a student in Cābridge. And published by I. C. Gent.* (London: Richarde Jones, 1579), STC 4283. For a description of one of these

poems in relation to "Cupido Conquered," see Lisle Cecil John, *The Eliza-bethan Sonnet Sequences: Studies in Conventional Conceits* (New York: Columbia Univ. Press, 1938), pp. 49, 225, n. 36.

45. By W[illiam?]. A[verell?]. (London: Richard Ihones, 1579), STC 982, in *Three Collections of English Poetry of the Latter Part of the Sixteenth Century, London, 1578-9* (London: Roxburghe Club, 1844).

46. 219 ottava rima stanzas plus a thirty-six-line interpolation from Chau-cer: 1788 lines. The "Eglogs" as a group contain 654 fourteeners or 1,308 half-lines.

47. Peirce gives a thorough account of the poem, pp. 178–214, to which I am indebted. He hesitates to make a firm attribution, but his evidence in favor of Googe's authorship is incontrovertible. Joseph Haslewood summa-rizes and quotes from the poem in Sir Egerton Brydges, *The British Bibliog-rapher*, 4 vols. (London: for R. Triphook by T. Bensley, 1810–14), II: 618–34.

48. The title he gave to his 1568 translation of Dominicus Mancinus's pop-ular *Libellus de quattuor virtutibus*.

49. See G. R. Owst, *Literature and the Pulpit in Medieval England*, 2nd ed. (Oxford: Basil Blackwell, 1961), pp. 67–76, 177–78. For further examples and discussion of the literary use of the figure, see Hugo Rahner, S. J., *Greek Myths and Christian Mystery*, trans. Brian Battershaw (New York: Harper, 1963; German ed. Zurich: Rhein-Verlag, 1957), pp. 328–90; B. Nellish, "The Allegory of Guyon's Voyage: An Interpretation," *ELH* XXX (1963): 89–106, passim; Kathleen Williams, "Spenser: Some Uses of the Sea and the Storm-tossed Ship," *Research Opportunities in Renaissance Drama* XIII–XIV (1970–71): 135–42; and Jerome S. Dees, "The Ship Conceit in *The Faerie Queene*: 'Conspicuous Allusion' and Poetic Structure," *Studies in Philology* LXXII (1975): 208–25. The related concept of man's life as an exile's voyage to his proper home in heaven is treated by G. V. Smithers in "The Meaning of *The Seafarer* and *The Wanderer*," *Medium Aevum* XXVI (1957): 137–53; XXVII (1959): 1–22. Significantly, the medieval poems and the tissue of traditional ideas and figures from which they are said by Smithers to emerge have an eschatological focus rather than the ethical concern of Googe.

50. In citing "The Ship of Safegarde," I refer to stanzas and signature numbers.

51. Paul condemns idolatry in I Corinthians 8 and elsewhere. The idea of Paul as a pilot is developed in St. John Chrysostom's homily on Acts 26:30–32 (Homily LIII), in which Paul's powers of prophecy are credited with bringing his ship and shipmates safely to port. See *A Select Library of the Nicene and Post-Nicene Fathers*, ed. Philip Schaff (Grand Rapids, Mich.: Wm. B. Eerdmans, 1956; orig. pub. 1889), XI, 314–19. See also *Patrologiae Cursus Completus . . . Series Graeca Prior*, ed. J. P. Migne (Paris: Migne, 1862), LX, 367–74. The whole homily is an elaborate exposition of a sea voy-age that takes on definite symbolic overtones similar to those Googe employs.

A few stanzas earlier (157; sig. D4v) Googe mentions Chrysostom by name as a previous sailor on the "brittell seas" near heresy, and attributes to him a sure-fire way to tell a heretic from a true believer: heretics, like wolves in sheep's clothing, are cruel to their enemies, while true believers have no need to be. Chrysostom treats this idea in his Homily XXIV on II Corinthians 11:13 (Schaff, 1st ser. XII, 390–94; Migne, *PG*, LXI, 563–70).

52. Googe may have seen Andrea Alciati's emblem of the Sirens, for example. Cf. Arthur Henkel and Albrecht Schöne, *Emblemata* (Stuttgart: J. B. Metzler, 1967), p. 1697. Googe's procedure in "The Ship of Safegarde" parallels the yoking of symbolic images and explanatory moral commentary in the emblem books.

53. Peirce calls this section the heart of the poem. See pp. 189–97.

54. See Rahner, pp. 328–90, who argues that the figure developed from a combination of the strong impression made by the dangers of sea travel on the mind of antiquity and the familiarity and richness of Odysseus' travels as told by Homer and allegorized by both pagan and Christian commentators. See also Don Cameron Allen, *Mysteriously Meant: The Rediscovery of Pagan Symbolism and Allegorical Interpretation in the Renaissance* (Baltimore: Johns Hopkins Press, 1970), pp. 84–96; John M. Steadman, *The Lamb and the Elephant: Ideal Imitation and the Context of Renaissance Allegory* (San Marino, Calif.: Huntington Library, 1974), p. 141, n. 2; and Nellish, ELH XXX (1963): 89–106.

55. Cf. the garden of Voluptuousness in Palingenius's "Gemini," discussed above, p. 38.

56. Allen, *Mysteriously Meant*, p. 90. See also Hallett Smith, *Elizabethan Poetry* (Cambridge, Mass.: Harvard Univ. Press, 1952), pp. 306–10, and Rahner, pp. 328–90.

57. See Allen, *Mysteriously Meant*, p. 87, n. 11; Merritt Y. Hughes, "Spenser's Acrasia and the Circe of the Renaissance," *Journal of the History of Ideas* IV (1943): 381–99; Nellish, p. 90; and Rosemond Tuve, *Images and Themes in Five Poems by Milton* (Cambridge, Mass.: Harvard Univ. Press, 1957).

58. If Googe studied Santillana's work in general between his trip to Spain and 1569, he might have been inspired by the Spanish poet's *Infierno de los enamoradas*, with which this passage has some similarity. See Foster, pp. 55–64; Post, pp. 212–14.

59. Googe eschews the identification of Ulysses' mast with the cross developed by some medieval writers (see Rahner, pp. 371–90). To identify it as reason suits his Protestantism and his theme that avoidance of shipwreck is a matter of personal moral choice, but it conflicts with his idea that no one can resist the Sirens' song.

60. See Nellish, pp. 89–106.

61. Nellish offers a detailed account of this episode within its traditional context. There are similarities between some of the places visited by Guyon

and by Googe, especially between the island of Fleshly Pleasure and the Bower of Bliss. See Peirce for detailed comparisons, pp. 194–200.

62. *Elizabethan and Metaphysical Imagery*, pp. 107–108.

63. Wilson, ed. Bowers, p. 198. Googe thus writes what Michael Murrin calls *rhetorical allegory* rather than *poetic allegory*. The latter type, characteristic of *The Faerie Queene*, he argues, gives value to truth by obscuring it from the understanding of all but an elite few; the former, characteristic of popular morality plays and Puritan polemics, having the same intention as a public sermon, makes no effort to conceal its simple moral persuasions. See *The Veil of Allegory* (Chicago: Univ. of Chicago Press, 1969), esp. pp. 3–20.

64. Among many casual uses of the figure in the Renaissance, it is worth noting that the Redcrosse Knight's labors are seen in retrospect as a voyage across a "sea of deadly daungers" (see *FQ* I, xxi, 15, 17). See also p. 100 below.

65. Sir Thomas Elyot, *The Boke Named the Gouernour* (1531), ed. H. H. S. Croft (London: Kegan Paul, Trench, & Co., 1883), I, 70.

66. Peirce praises Googe's use of certain effective images (pp. 187–89), and finds "some passages which suggest a poetic virtuosity not entirely to be scorned" (p. 184).

Chapter Five

1. *Sir Fulke Greville's Life of Sir Philip Sidney . . . (1652)*, ed. Nowell Smith (Oxford: Clarendon Press, 1907), p. 224.

2. *Zodiake*, 1565, sigs. °6v, (‡)4.

3. See J. E. L. Oulton, "Rufinus's Translation of the Church History of Eusebius," *Journal of Theological Studies* XXX (1929): 150–74. I have consulted a photo-copy of *Ecclesiastica Historia diui Eusebii: et Ecclesiastica historia gentis anglorum venerabilis Bede* (Strassburg: George Husner, 1500), hereinafter referred to as Rufinus, 1500; but in quoting I follow the modernized orthography of the edition of Rufinus by Theodore Mommsen in Eusebius, *Kirchengeschichte*, ed. Eduard Schwartz (Leipzig: J. C. Hinrichs Buchhandlung, 1903).

4. Rufinus, 1500, sigs. E3–E4; cf. Eusebius, *The Ecclesiastical History*, ed. and trans. Kirsopp Lake, Loeb Classical Library (London: William Heinemann, 1926), I, 343–55.

5. Rufinus: " . . . ita ut pedem laederet praeceps actus" (IV, 15, 16; Mommsen, I, 343).

6. Rufinus's interpolation appears in Book VII, chapter 25, which corresponds to Book VII, chapter 28 of Lake. His version of the story differs from that in Gregory of Nyssa's life of St. Gregory the Wonder Worker (Migne, *PG*, 46: 914–18) and from that in the independent anonymous Latin life as well. See W. Telfer, "The Latin *Life* of St Gregory Thaumaturgus," *Journal of Theological Studies* XXXI (1929–30): 142–55, 354–62.

7. On Bale's connections with Naogeorgus, see Charles H. Herford, *Studies in the Literary Relations of England and Germany in the Sixteenth Century* (Cambridge: Cambridge Univ. Press, 1886), pp. 131–38; Honor C. McCusker, *John Bale: Dramatist and Antiquary* (Freeport, N.Y.: Books for Libraries Press, 1971; orig. pub. 1942), pp. 94–95; and (for a negative view on the question of influence) Thora Balslev Blatt, *The Plays of John Bale: A Study of Ideas, Technique and Style* (Copenhagen: G. E. C. Gad, 1969), pp. 164–81.

8. The *Regnum Papisticum* was published in Basel in 1553 and issued in revised form in 1559. Googe used the later edition (see Peirce, p. 95, n. 2). The *Agricultura Sacra* was published in Basel (1550). For Bale's life and opinions, see McCusker, pp. 1–28, and Blatt, pp. 9–19.

9. *The Popish Kingdome* was printed in London by Henrie Denham for Richard Watkins in 1570 and was not reprinted until 1880 (see Chapter 1, note 10). It was reprinted again in 1972 by Johnson Reprint Co. Neither reprint contains "The Spirituall Husbandrie." The fourth book and part of the third are included in *Phillip Stubbes's Anatomy of the Abuses in England in Shakespeare's Youth, A.D. 1583*, ed. Frederick J. Furnivall (London: New Shakspere Society, 1877–79), pp. 323–48.

10. See Roy Pascal, *German Literature in the Sixteenth and Seventeenth Centuries* (New York: Barnes and Noble, 1968), pp. 63–64; see also pp. 213–14. Cf. Herford, pp. xxv, 129–31; Fritz Wiener, *Naogeorgus im England der Reformationszeit* (Berlin: [n.p.], 1907), pp. 51–66; and *The Letters of Stephen Gardiner*, ed. James Arthur Muller (Westport, Conn.: Greenwood Press, 1970; orig. pub. Cambridge: Cambridge Univ. Press, 1933), pp. 129–40. Further information on Naogeorgus, whose birthdate is variously given as 1505, 1508, and 1511, and who died in 1563, may be found in Herford, pp. 93, 120–24, and in Hans-Gert Roloff, "Thomas Naogeorgs *Judas*—ein Drama der Reformationszeit," *Archiv für das Studium der Neuren Sprachen und Literaturen* CCVIII (1971): 81–101.

11. Besides Furnivall, see Hone, *Every-Day Book;* John Brand, *Observations on Popular Antiquities*, ed. Sir Henry Ellis (London: Charles Knight, 1841–42); and Karl Young, *The Drama of the Medieval Church* (Oxford: Clarendon Press, 1933), I, 139–40; II, 528–34.

12. See Wiener, pp. 114–31, and Peirce, pp. 98, 102–104.

13. Wiener describes the original and Googe's translation, pp. 132–39. See Herford, p. 121, for the suggestion that Naogeorgus meant the work as a Christian parallel to Vergil's *Georgics*.

14. The Latin is *Christophori Ballistae Parhisiensis in Podagrā concertatio, ad Reuerendissimum in Christo patrem, illustrissimumque principem, Dominum Philippum de Platea, Sedunensem Episcopum. Adiectus est dialogus inter Podagram & Christophorum Ballistam. Ad tria tendo* (Zurich?, 1525? or 1528?). Information on the author, on the poems, their tradition, and the translation, has been compiled by Robert Schuler in the introduction

and notes to his critical edition of the first of the two poems in *Three Renaissance Scientific Poems*, No. 5 of *Studies in Philology* LXXV (1978), pp. 67–107. I am grateful to Professor Schuler for letting me see the text of his commentary in advance of publication, and I am indebted to him in the pages that follow. To the ascription of this translation to Googe in Kennedy, *Dictionary of Anonymous and Pseudonymous Literature*, IV, 285, which was supported by Peirce, Schuler adds his endorsement, along with some further evidence of contact between Googe and Masters as servants of Cecil.

Peirce's account of the work (pp. 41–42, 154–57, 159–75) includes a comparison of the translation with the original Latin that reveals Googe's "characteristic fidelity to the language and figures of his original" (p. 162) and notes instances of his habitual diction and phraseology.

15. Schuler shows the main sources to be Pliny's *Natural History* and the *Materia Medica* of Dioscorides Pedanius.

16. He does delete a discussion of the relative immunity of menstruating women to the gout (see Peirce, p. 165).

17. *Rei rusticae libri quatuor, vniuersam rusticam disciplinam complectentes, vna cum appendice oraculorum cornidas adiecta. Item, de venatione, aucupio atque piscatione compendium* (Cologne: Iohannes Burckmann, 1570). On Heresbach, see *Neue Deutsche Biographie* (Berlin: Duncker & Humblot, 1969), VII, 606–607. See also the facsimile edition of the first book of *Rei rusticae* by Wilhelm Abel, with a facing page German translation by Helmut Dreitzel, *Vier Bücher über Landwirtschaft, Band I, Vom Landblau* (Meisenheim: A. Hain, 1970).

18. In a line added to the *Husbandry* he remarks on "Linconshyre, a countrey replenished with Gentlemen of good houses, and good house keepers" (sig. Y3v).

19. Googe inadvertently omits a half-dozen names cited by Heresbach in his similar list and adds one of his own, "Tragus," to be discussed below. The contributions of some of the Englishmen listed are specified in the text; some, like Tusser, seem to be mentioned out of courtesy only. The idea that the names may represent "missing Tudor books on farming" has been demolished by Peirce (pp. 40–41). Googe also cites British authorities he neglects to list, including Reynolde (Reginald) Scot's *A Perfite Platforme of a Hoppe Garden* (1574) and Thomas Blundeville's *The Fower Chiefyst Offices Belonging to Horsemanshippe* (1565, 1566)—see sigs. H8v, P2v.

20. I.e., John Fitzherbert's *Boke of Husbandry*, published under that and other titles ten times between 1523 and 1568 (STC 10994–11003). To his friend and later commander in Ireland, Sir Nicholas Malbie, Googe attributes an "infallible" treatment for horses (sig. Q3v) taken from Malbie's *A Plaine and Easie Way to Remedie a Horse that is Foundered in his Feete* (1576).

21. I.e., Girolamo Cardano (1501–1576), author of *Ars curandi parva* (Basel: Ex Officina Henricpetrina, 1566); Pietro Andrea Mattioli (1500–1577), whose commentary on Dioscorides's *Materia Medica* (Venice: Vincenzo Val-

grisi, 1568) was widely disseminated in various versions (cf. the facsimile edition, Rome: [n.p.], 1970); and Hieronymus Bock (1498–1554), author of *De stirpivm . . . commentarium libri tres* (Strassburg: V. Rihelius, 1552).

22. Cf. Bock, sig. Cc3 (p. 405). The style and contents of the two drawings are identical, but the various parts of the plant are differently arranged.

23. Webbe, sig. F1v.

24. See Rowland E. Prothero, Lord Ernle, *English Farming, Past and Present* (New York: Benjamin Blom, 1972; orig pub. 1917), pp. 89, 99–100.

25. On the cat and the malt heap, see Tilley, C177 (p. 88).

26. See Foster, *Santillana*. See also José Amador de los Rios, ed., *Obras . . . de Santillana* (Madrid: José Rodriquez, 1852); Marcelino Menéndez Pelayo, "Estudio Preliminar" to his selected, modernized edition of the *Proverbios* (Madrid: Atlas, 1944); Rafael Lapesa, *La obra literaria del Marqués de Santillana* (Madrid: Insula, 1957); Mario Schiff, *La bibliothèque du Marquis de Santillane* (Paris: Librarie Émile Bouillon, 1905); and, on Santillana's humanist predilections, Arnold Reichenberger, "The Marqués de Santillana and the Classical Tradition," *Ibero-romania* I (1969): 5–34, and Miguel Garci-Gómez, "The Reaction against Medieval Romances: Its Spanish Forerunners," *Neophilologus* LX (1976) 220–32.

27. Diaz wrote a *Diálogo é razonamiento en la muerte del Marqués de Santillana*, printed in *Opusculos Literarios de los siglos XIV á XVI*, ed. A. Paz y Melia, Sociedad de Bibliófilos Españoles, vol. XIX (Madrid, 1892), pp. 245–360, a commentary on the adages of "Seneca" (Publilius Syrus) (see note 30, below), and prefaces to other works he translated for the Marqués. See Schiff, passim. See also Paz y Melia, pp. xiii–xiv.

28. See Schiff, pp. xxiii, xxvi, and José Simon Díaz, *Bibliografia de la literatura Hispánica* (Madrid: Consejo Superior de Investigaciones Científicas, 1950–), III, 693. See also *Los Proverbios con su Glosa*, Incunables Poeticos Castellanos, XI (Valencia: Artes Gráficas Soler, 1965), a facsimile of the Seville edition of 1494.

29. See Pulgar, *Claros varones de Castilla*, ed. Robert Brian Tate (Oxford: Clarendon Press, 1971), esp. pp. li–lii; see also *Biographie Universelle* (Paris: Michaud Frères, 1811–28), XXXVI, 313–14.

30. *Prouerbios y Sentencias de Lucio Anneo Seneca, y de Don Yñigo Lopez de Mendoça, Marques de Santillana. Glosados por el Doctor Pedro Diaz de Toledo* (Antwerp: Iuan Steelsio, 1552); Simon Díaz No. 3450. Googe did not translate any of the first ("Senecan") part of the volume nor the introductions by Diaz and Santillana that precede the second part. The 1552 edition varies from the MS.-based text in the *Obras* in ways similar to the printed text of 1494, as in the omission of the ninety-third proverb. Googe always follows 1552 when it differs from 1494, as in the omission of the seventh proverb plus some surrounding prose, in errors in the headings and numeration of chapters, and in the quotation of four lines from Petrarch (see below, p. 115). Finally, a passage on military discipline in Pulgar's portrait of San-

tillana (Tate, ed., pp. 22–23) is absent both from 1552 and from Googe's translation.

31. J. B. Trend, ed., *Prose and Verse [by the] Marqués de Santillana* (London: Dolphin Bookshop, 1940), p. xvi.

32. According to Pulgar, but see Pelayo, pp. 21–22.

33. See *Obras*, ed. Amador de los Rios, pp. 21–22.

34. Cf. his chapters "of Duetie to Parents" and "of Age" (fols. 103–112). Diaz seconds him in the gloss, fols. 24–27v, 109–112.

35. I cite the proverbs as numbered by Googe. See note 30, above.

36. As Googe recognized them to be, rather than true popular proverbs, in his epistle dedicatory.

37. Foster shares this judgment (pp. 69–70, 72).

38. In his prologue, Santillana disclaimed any attempt at originality (*Obras*, ed. Amador de los Rios, p. 26; cf. Schiff, p. lxxxi).

39. See Schiff, p. lxxxi: "ils restent sans effort dans l'oreille de qui les a entendus."

40. Googe's marginalia are sparse, some perhaps having been omitted by the printer, as he seems to imply in the dedicatory epistle. He may have intended to enter more objections. There are no marginalia in 1552.

41. Durling, ed. and trans., *Petrarch's Lyric Poems*, p. 204 (No. 102).

42. See Peirce, pp. 141, 145–46, for a similar opinion.

43. On Santillana, see Foster, p. 69. Diaz is more ambitious and coherent in his *Diálogo*.

44. See Schiff, pp. xxiii, xxxvi.

45. Printed by Robert Robinson for Richard Watkins, London, 1587. "The Epistle" is signed "Aluingham this 14. of August, 1587 . . . B.G." Peirce shows that this work and the *Gout* may be attributed to Googe as an indivisible pair (pp. 154–57).

46. A copy of the original is in the British Museum: Bertholdus (Andreas), *Terrae sigillatae, nuper in Germania repertae, vires atque virtutes admirandae, eiusque administrandae ac vsurpandae ratio* (Frankfort: C. Rab, 1583).

Selected Bibliography

PRIMARY SOURCES

1. Renaissance Editions of Googe's Original Works

A prefatory poem in Nilus [Cabasilas], *A Briefe Treatise, Conteynynge a playne and fruitfull declaration of the Popes vsurped Primacye*. Trans. Thomas Gressop. London: Henry Sutton for Rafe Newbery, 1560. STC 4325.

Eglogs Epytaphes, and Sonettes. Newly written by Barnabe Googe. London: Thomas Colwell, for Raffe Newbery, 1563. STC 12048.

A newe Booke called the Shippe of safegarde, wrytten by G. B. London: W. Seres, 1569. STC 12049.

A prose prefatory epistle to *Allarme to England,* by Barnabe Riche. London: Henry Middleton for C. B., [1578]. STC 20978.

(Other original poems appear in the translation of Palingenius listed below. All the translations contain some prefatory prose as well.)

2. Renaissance Editions of Googe's Translations

[ARBALESTE, CHRISTOPHE]. *The Overthrow of the Gout / Written in Latin verse, by Doctor Christopher Balista*. Trans. B. G. London: Abraham Veale, 1577. RSTC 1312.5.

BERTHOLDUS, ANDREAS. *The Wonderfull and strange effect and vertues of a new Terra Sigillata lately found out in Germanie*. Trans. B. G. London: Robert Robinson for Richard Watkins, 1587. STC 1970.

HERESBACH, CONRAD. *Fovre Bookes of Husbandry*. Trans. Barnabe Googe. London: Richard Watkins, 1577. STC 13196. The book was subsequently issued by John Wight in 1578 (STC 13197) and 1586 (STC 13198), by T. Este in 1596 (STC 13199), by T. Wight in 1601 (STC 13200), and by T. S[nodham] for Richard More in 1614 (STC 13201). Most of Googe's text is included in the revision by Gervase Markham, *The Whole Art of Husbandry,* printed by T. C. for Richard More in 1631 (STC 13202).

NAOGEORGUS, THOMAS. *The Popish Kingdome, or reigne of Antichrist*. Trans. Barnabe Googe. London: Henrie Denham for Richarde Watkins, 1570. STC 15011.

PALINGENIUS, MARCELLUS. *The Firste thre Bokes of the most christiā Poet Marcellus Palingenius, called the Zodyake of lyfe*. Trans. Barnabe Googe. London: Iohn Tisdale, for Rafe Newberye, 1560. STC 19148. Subsequent editions of *The Zodiake of Life* were *The firste syxe bokes,*

. . . Iohn Tisdale, for Rafe Newbery, 1561 (STC 19149); *The Zodiake of Life*, Henry Denham, for Rafe Newberye, 1565 (STC 19150); *The Zodiake of life*, for Raufe Newberie, 1576; and a reprint of that edition by Robert Robinson, 1588. Apparatus varies: 1560 and 1561 have an explanatory appendix; 1576 and 1588 have marginalia and an index.

SANTILLANA, IÑIGO LOPES DE MENDOZA, MARQUÉS OF. *The Prouerbes of the noble and woorthy souldier Sir Iames Lopez de Mendoza Marques of Santillana, with the Paraphrase of D. Peter Diaz of Toledo.* Trans. Barnabe Googe. London: Richarde Watkins, 1579. Contains "The life of Sir Iames Lopez de Mendoza, Marques of Santilliana," prose, translated from the Spanish of Fernando del Pulgar.

3. Modern Editions and Reprints of Original Works

Eglogs, Epytaphes, and Sonettes 1563. Ed. Edward Arber. Westminster: Constable, 1895; orig. pub. 1871. An emended reprint, but in roman rather than gothic type, with an introduction and a compilation of biographical documents and information.

Selected Poems of Barnabe Googe. Ed. Alan Stephens. Denver: Alan Swallow, 1961. Modern-spelling transcriptions of most of the short poems from *Eglogs, Epytaphes, and Sonettes*, with notes and a valuable critical introduction.

Eglogs Epytaphes, and Sonettes (1563). Introd. Frank B. Fieler. Gainesville, Fla.: Scholars' Facsimiles & Reprints, 1968. A photo-lithographic reproduction with occasional inked-in emendations and a brief factual and critical introduction.

4. Modern Editions and Reprints of Translations

The Popish Kingdome, or reigne of Antichrist. Translated by Barnabe Googe, 1570. Ed. R. C. Hope. London: privately printed, 1880. Omits "The Spirituall Husbandrie"; contains a biographical introduction.

The Zodiake of Life by Marcellus Palingenius. Introd. Rosemond Tuve. New York: Scholars' Facsimiles & Reprints, 1947. A photo-lithographic reproduction of the 1576 edition with an appendix of prefatory materials from other editions and an extensive introductory essay.

Fovre Bookes of Husbandry, by Conrad Heresbach. New York: Da Capo Press, 1971. No apparatus. A photo-lithographic reproduction.

The popish kingdom or reign of Antichrist written in Latin verse by Thomas Naogeorgus translated by B. Googe 1570. Introd. Peter Davison. New York: Johnson Reprint Co., 1972. Omits "The Spirituall Husbandrie"; contains a brief headnote only. A photo-lithographic reproduction.

"The Overthrow of the Gout," in Robert Schuler, *Three Renaissance Scientific Poems.* No. 5 of *Studies in Philology* LXXV (1978), pp. 67–107.

SECONDARY SOURCES

(Only substantial studies directly about Googe's writings are listed; others
are mentioned in the notes. See also the introductions to the modern editions
and reprints listed above.)

HARRISON, T. P., JR. "Googe's *Eglogs* and Montemayor's *Diana.*" *University
of Texas Studies in English* V (1925); 68–78. Studies the Spanish influence on eclogues five, six, and seven.
PANOFSKY, RICHARD JACOB. "A Descriptive Study of English Mid-Tudor Short
Poetry, 1557–1577." Diss. University of California, Santa Barbara, 1975,
pp. 36, 77–78, 90–92, 131–38, 140, 145–46, 157, 165–68, 230–31, 234–
35. Googe's style and techniques as part of the early Elizabethan mode.
PARNELL, PAUL E. "Barnabe Googe: A Puritan in Arcadia." *Journal of
English and Germanic Philology* LX (1961): 273–81. An important
study of the "Eglogs" as a homily against love.
PEIRCE, BROOKE. "Barnabe Googe: Poet and Translator." Diss. Harvard, 1954.
The best scholarly account of Googe. Includes a full biography and discussions of all works, translated and original.
PETERSON, DOUGLAS L. *The English Lyric from Wyatt to Donne: A History
of the Plain and Eloquent Styles.* Princeton: Princeton University Press,
1967, pp. 134–45. Explications of several short poems with attention to
their rhetorical structures.
SHEIDLEY, WILLIAM E. "A Timely Anachronism: Tradition and Theme in Barnabe Googe's 'Cupido Conquered.'" *Studies in Philology* LXIX (1972):
150–66. A revised and abbreviated form of this essay is included in
Chapter 3 of the present study.

Index

147